KINTORE SCHOOL
KINTORE
ABERDEENSHIRE

D1324889

Primary
Maths
in Action

Pupil Book

Irene Hogg

Robin Howat

David McNulty

Eddie Mullan

Ken Nisbet

Sandra White

nelson thornes

Text © I. Hogg, R. Howat, D. McNulty, E. Mullan, K. Nisbet, S. White 2004
Original illustrations © Nelson Thornes Ltd 2004

The right of I. Hogg, R. Howat, D. McNulty, E. Mullan, K. Nisbet and S. White to be identified as authors of this work has been asserted by them in accordance with the Copyright, Designs and Patents Act 1988.

All rights reserved. No part of this publication may be reproduced or transmitted in any form or by any means, electronic or mechanical, including photocopy, recording or any information storage and retrieval system, without permission in writing from the publisher or under licence from the Copyright Licensing Agency Limited, of 90 Tottenham Court Road, London W1T 4LP.

Any person who commits any unauthorised act in relation to this publication may be liable to criminal prosecution and civil claims for damages.

Published in 2004 by:
Nelson Thornes Ltd
Delta Place
27 Bath Road
CHELTENHAM
GL53 7TH
United Kingdom

05 06 / 10 9 8 7 6 5 4 3 2

A catalogue record for this book is available from the British Library

ISBN 0–7487–7705–9

Design, Illustration and Typesetting by J&L Composition, Filey, North Yorkshire

Printed in Great Britain by Scotprint

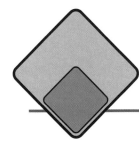# Contents

Block 4

Whole Numbers

Some numbers are really big!

Age of the Earth
4 600 000 000 years

The distance of Pluto from the Sun
7 364 000 000 km

Area of the Pacific Ocean
165 400 000 km²

Speed of light
299 800 000 metres per second

 ## Looking Back

1. The number of primary school pupils in Scotland last year was 438 082.
   The number of secondary school pupils was 302 821.

   Write both numbers in words.

2. The number of visitors to Edinburgh Zoo ten years ago was *four hundred and ninety-eight thousand, seven hundred and ten.*
   The number of visitors last year was *five hundred and thirty thousand, four hundred and five.*

   Write both numbers in figures.

3. The 2001 Census estimated the number of people in Scotland aged over 90 as 29 114.
   What would the number be if there had been:

   a 10 more   b 10 000 more   c 1000 more   d 100 less   e 200 less?

4. This table shows the number of people living in Highland in 2001 in certain age groups.

Age Group	0–4	5–9	10–14	15–19	20–24	25–29
Population	11 363	13 070	13 780	12 122	9995	11 264

Put these populations in order, starting with the biggest.

5. Round the populations in question **4** to the nearest:

   a 10   b 100   c 1000.

6. Using each of these digits once in each number, what is:

   a the largest number you can make
   b the smallest number you can make
   c the largest odd number you can make
   d the smallest even number you can make
   e the largest number divisible by 5 you can make?

   8 2 3 7 5

7. a How many more pople live in Eastmere than in Westsea?
   b What is the total population of the two towns?
   c 3782 females live in Westsea. How many males live there?
   d 4689 females live in Eastmere. How many males live there?
   e Are there more females or more males in total in the two towns? How many more?

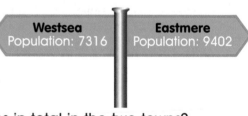

Westsea
Population: 7316

Eastmere
Population: 9402

8. 4863 CDs of *Marty's Greatest Hits* were sold on the first day of release. How much money was made from these sales?

9. How many weeks are in 1000 days?

10. A garage makes a profit of 9p on every litre of petrol sold.

   a One week the garage sold 9875 litres of petrol. Calculate its profit.
   b The following week the garage made a profit of £1206. How many litres of petrol did the garage sell that week?

11. The table shows the number of units of gas used by the Gordon family in each quarter of last year.

	Jan–Mar	Apr–Jun	Jul–Sep	Oct–Dec
Number of units	2315	1266	895	1982

    a How many units of gas did they use altogether?
    b Each unit of gas cost 8p. Calculate:
      i the cost of gas for each quarter
     ii the cost of gas for the year.

12. Calculate the OUT number for each of these number machines.

2   Big Numbers

millions			thousands					
hundreds	tens	units	hundreds	tens	units	hundreds	tens	units
3	7	2	5	4	1	9	6	8

Three hundred and seventy-two million,
five hundred and forty-one thousand,
nine hundred and sixty-eight.

300 000 000
70 000 000
2 000 000
500 000
40 000
1 000
900
60
8
372 541 968

1. In Britain last year:

    a the number of primary school pupils was 4 724 940
    b the number of secondary school pupils was 3 354 575
    c the number of students at university was 2 024 170.

Write these three numbers in words.

2. a The total forest area in
   Scotland in 1990 was
   1 120 625 hectares.
   b In 2000, it was 1 318 750
   hectares.
   c In Britain in 2000, the figure
   was 2 827 500 hectares.

   Write these three numbers in
   words.

3. a Last year, *one million, two hundred
     and four thousand, eight hundred*
     people visited Edinburgh Castle.
   b In the same year, there were *one
     million, three thousand, six hundred
     and fifty* visitors to Kelvingrove
     Art Gallery and Museum.

   Write both numbers in figures.

4. Write these three numbers in figures:

   a In 1999, *one million, thirty-one thousand, eight hundred and
     seventy-five* tonnes of potatoes were produced in Scotland.
   b In 2000, the figure was *one million, one hundred and fourteen
     thousand, two hundred and fifty* tonnes.
   c In Britain in 2000, *six million, six hundred and eleven thousand and fifty*
     tonnes of potatoes were produced.

5. In Scotland in 2001, there were 584 012 children under ten years old. Write
   down the number if there had been:

   a 500 more   b 10 000 more   c 1000 less   d 6000 more   e 13 less.

6. The total number of visitors to Scotland from overseas last year was
   1 805 750.

   Write down the number if there had
   been:

   a 500 less   b 10 000 more
   c 300 more   d 200 000 more
   e 10 000 less.

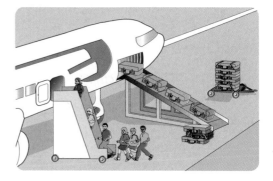

7. The table gives Census figures for the population of Aberdeen:

	1961	1971	1981	1991	2001
Population	205 789	212 073	203 965	190 178	210 304

Write the five population figures in order, starting with the smallest.

8. Over a five-year period the numbers of vehicles each year crossing the River Clyde on the Erskine Bridge were:

6 809 750   6 865 975   7 420 250

6 622 500   7 401 750

Put these numbers of vehicles in order, starting with the lowest.

9. Using each of these digits once in each number, make:

a the largest number
b the smallest number
c the largest odd number
d the smallest odd number
e the smallest even number
f the largest even number.

10. Using each of these tiles once in each number, make:

a the largest number
b the smallest number
c the second largest number
d the largest even number.

3	5	4	1

8	5	4

Challenge

8	8	8	3	8	3

Make all the 6-digit numbers you can with these digits.

Put all your 6-digit numbers in order, starting with the smallest.

3 Using Numbers

◇ A ─────────────────────────────────

1. Calculate:

   a 3618 + 4769   b 5273 + 2768   c 8746 + 4596   d 7362 − 3165

   e 8153 − 1436   f 5231 − 2657   g 6053 − 2768   h 8888 × 7

   i 9657 × 6   j 7884 ÷ 9   k 6312 ÷ 8   l 7770 ÷ 6

2. Calculate:

   a 3462 + 5788 + 4763   b 5636 + 3965 − 7834

3. Find the value of:

   a 6873 ÷ 8   b 7064 ÷ 9   c 6666 ÷ 7

4. Add:

   3162 + 89 + 753 + 8 + 4762

5. A school library has 7415 fiction books, 2838 non-fiction books and 364 reference books.

   a How many books are there altogether?
   b How many more fiction books are there than non-fiction books?

6. Eight friends have an equal share of a £7784 lottery prize.
   What is each friend's share?

7. 7586 people each paid £9 to see
   Rovers play City.
   How much money was paid in total?

8. a What is the cost of 5347 units of electricity at 8 pence per unit?
   b A gas bill came to £173·40. Each unit of gas cost 6 pence.
      How many units of gas were used?

9. These are the charges for a round of golf on the course at Darley.

   In July, 3946 weekday tickets were sold and 948 tickets were sold at the weekend. How much money was made from the sale of tickets in July?

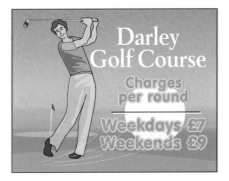

10. The table shows the number of people paying for the main activities at The Centrum Leisure Centre in March and the prices of these activities.

	Skating	Go-Karting	Curling	Quad Bikes
Number	4653	3716	1089	2876
Price (£)	6	8	7	9

a How much money was made from:
  i skating ii go-karting iii curling iv quad bikes?

b What was the total number of people who paid for these activities?
c How much money was made altogether from the four activities?
d The Centrum made £9702 from the sale of Family Movie tickets, which cost £7 each. How many of these tickets were sold?

 B

1. Find the value of:

   a 9999 + 9899   b 4500 − 1834   c 7000 − 3614   d 9000 − 3527
   e 10 000 − 4872   f 9989 × 9   g 8888 ÷ 9   h 5555 ÷ 7

2. Calculate:

   a 2364 × 2   b 2364 × 20   c 2364 × 200   d 85 000 ÷ 5
   e 85 000 ÷ 50   f 85 000 ÷ 500   g 837 × 6   h 837 × 60
   i 837 × 600   j 9100 ÷ 7   k 9100 ÷ 70   l 9100 ÷ 700
   m 6127 × 40   n 3472 × 80   o 5163 × 700   p 9274 × 500

3. The diagram shows the distances between four cities.

   a How much shorter is it to fly from London to Sydney via Beijing than via Johannesburg?
   b Sal cannot get a direct flight from Johannesburg to Beijing. How much shorter is it to fly there via London than via Sydney?

London 5054 miles Beijing 5689 miles 5640 miles Johannesburg 7601 miles Sydney

4. In the Great Hill Run for charity all runners ran 9 km, 8 km or 7 km. 2805 runners ran 9 km, 3672 ran 8 km and 1089 ran 7 km.

   a How many attempted the Great Hill Run?
   b The sponsors agreed to pay 1p to charity for every kilometre run. How much do the sponsors have to pay?

5. The Noel Card Company sells boxes of luxury Christmas cards to shops. Last Christmas they sold 8637 boxes of cards at £7 per box.

   a How much money did they make?
   b There are 60 cards to a box. How many cards did they sell altogether?

6. Which number is bigger, and by how much?

   a 8888×70 or 7777×80
   b 9990×60 or 6660×90
   c 5505×70 or 7707×50

7. Danny's dad's car can travel 9 km on one litre of petrol when driven on the motorway.
   It usually travels 6 km on one litre of petrol when driven in the city.

   a How many litres of petrol are needed for 5000 km of motorway driving plus 2000 km of city driving?
   b How much did Danny's dad spend on petrol if it cost 90p per litre?

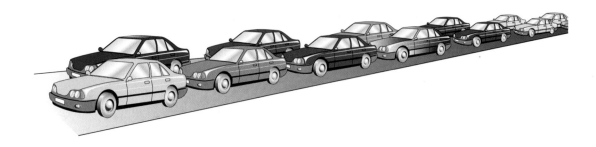

8. Listed below are the maximum distances of the planets in the solar system from the Sun.

Mercury	69 400 000 km
Venus	109 000 000 km
Earth	152 600 000 km
Mars	249 200 000 km
Jupiter	817 400 000 km
Saturn	1 512 000 000 km
Uranus	3 011 000 000 km
Neptune	4 543 000 000 km
Pluto	7 364 000 000 km

a Write the distances of the five planets furthest away from the Sun in words.

b How much nearer the Sun is:
   i   the Earth than Mars
   ii Mars than Jupiter
   iii Uranus than Saturn
   iv Pluto than Mercury?

Challenge

1. What is the smallest whole number that all of 1, 2, 3, 4, 5, 6, 7, 8 and 9 will divide into evenly?

2. Write in figures:

   a half a million   b three and a quarter million

   c ten and a half million.

3. Write in figures the number that is one less than:

   a half a million   b three and a quarter million

   c ten and a half million.

4. Write in figures:

   a 4 billion   b 10 billion   c half a billion   d a billion billion.

1 ▷ Looking Back

1. Use one of these words to describe each angle below: **acute**, **obtuse**, **right** or **straight**.

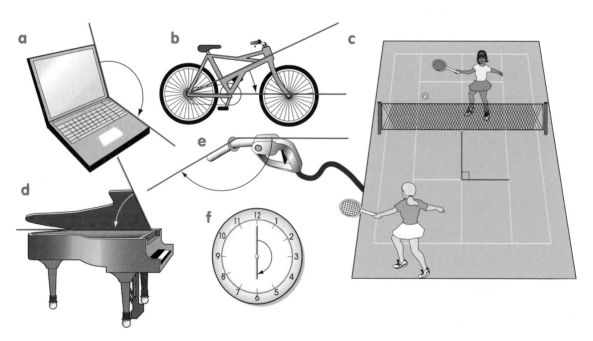

2. Which of the pictures in question **1** show the angle as a rotation and which as a shape?

3. Measure the size of each angle.

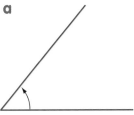 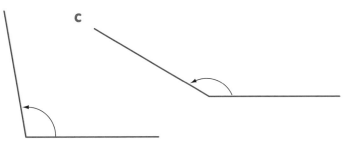

a   b   c

4. **a** **i** Draw an angle of 55°. Call it ∠ABC.
     ii Name the vertex of the angle.
     iii Name the arms of the angle.

   b **i** Draw an angle of 130°. Call it ∠LPF.
     ii Name the vertex of the angle.
     iii Name the arms of the angle.

2 Summing Angles

Angles that form a right angle are called complementary angles.
Complementary angles add up to 90°.

Example   ∠ABD forms a right angle with ∠DBC.
$$90 - 55 = 35$$
so ∠DBC = 35°.

35° is said to be the complement of 55°.

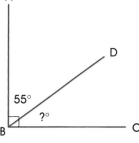

Angles that form a straight angle are called
supplementary angles.
Supplementary angles add up to 180°.

Example   ∠ABD forms a straight line with ∠DBC.
$$180 - 145 = 35$$
so ∠DBC = 35°.

35° is said to be the supplement
of 145°.

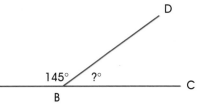

Angles that are bigger than 180° are called reflex angles.
Angles that form a complete revolution add up to 360°.

Example   ∠ABC forms a complete revolution with
reflex ∠ABC.
$$360 - 35 = 325$$
so reflex ∠ABC = 325°.

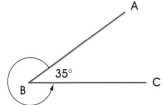

A

1. Calculate the marked angle in each diagram.

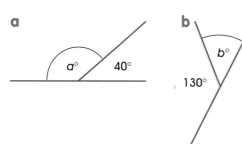

a

66°

a°

b

b° 42°

c

c°

77°

d

d° 53°

2. What is the complement of:

    a 65°   b 15°   c 5°   d 0°   e 45°?

3. ABCD is a square.

    a What is the size of ∠ABC?
    b ∠EAD = 60°. What is the size of ∠BAE?
       Give a reason for your answer.
    c What is the size of ∠EDC?

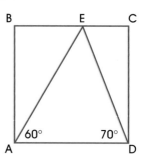

4. What is the supplement of:

    a 100°   b 55°   c 95°   d 10°   e 5°?

5. Calculate the marked angle in each diagram.

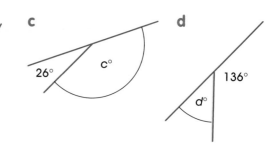

a

a° 40°

b

b°

130°

c

26° c°

d

136°

d°

6. a Name the supplement to ∠BEC
    b Calculate the size of ∠AEC.
    c What is the size of ∠ADC?

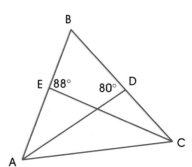

7. Calculate the size of each reflex angle.

a

b
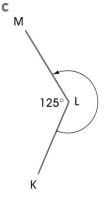

c
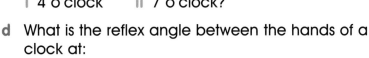

d
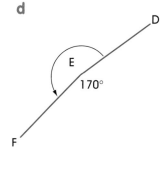

B

1. 360° make a revolution.

  a Into how many segments is the clock face divided?

  b What is the acute angle between the hands of a clock at:
    i 1 o'clock   **ii** 2 o'clock?

  c What is the obtuse angle between the hands of a clock at:
    i 4 o'clock   **ii** 7 o'clock?

  d What is the reflex angle between the hands of a clock at:
    i 1 o'clock   **ii** 2 o'clock   **iii** 4 o'clock   **iv** 7 o'clock?

2. Two straight lines AB and CD cross at E.

  a ∠AEC = 40°. Calculate the size of ∠AED.
  b Calculate the size of ∠DEB.
  c Comment on the sizes of ∠AEC and ∠DEB.

3. In the diagram, PQ and RS are straight lines crossing at T.

  a Calculate ∠PTS when ∠PTR is:
    i 30°   **ii** 50°   **iii** 60°   **iv** 65°.

  b Hence calculate ∠QTS when ∠PTR is:
    i 30°   **ii** 50°   **iii** 60°   **iv** 65°.

  c Comment on the sizes of ∠QTS and ∠PTR in each case.

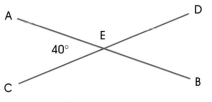

Vertically Opposite Angles

When two straight lines cross, the point where they cross is called a vertex.

Vertex

Questions **2** and **3** above show that the angles on opposite sides of the vertex are equal.

They are known as vertically opposite angles.

A

1.   Find each of the labelled angles by using vertically opposite angles.

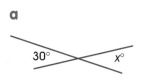

a

30° $x°$

b

$y°$ 88°

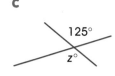

c

125°

$z°$

d

$q°$

2.   Using vertically opposite angles and supplementary angles, find all the angles in the diagram.

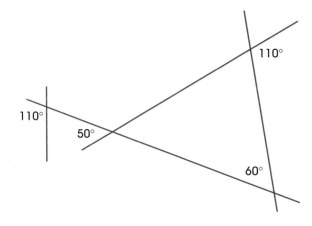

110°

110°

50°

60°

3.   Iona set up a deckchair.

   a   What size is ∠EBC when ∠ABD =
       i 23°   ii 32°   iii 12°?

   b   What size is ∠ABE when ∠ABD =
       i 50°   ii 43°   iii 4°?

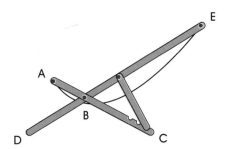

4. The legs of the ironing board can be altered to change the height.

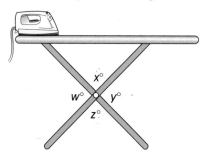

a What is the value of z when x =
  i 40°   ii 37°   iii 121°?

b Calculate the size of y when x =
  i 31°   ii 12°   iii 135°.

c Find the size of w when y =
  i 95°   ii 112°   iii 89°.

4 Angles and Parallels

When parallel lines are cut by another line, the pattern of angles made at each intersection is the same.

The line cutting across the parallels is called a transversal.

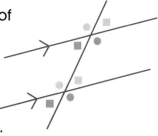

Angles related like this are called corresponding angles.

Example

AB is parallel to CD.
EF is a transversal cutting at G and H. ∠AGF = 40°.
Calculate all the angles in the diagram.
∠FGB is the supplement of ∠AGF, so ∠FGB = 140°.
∠BGE is vertically opposite ∠AGF, so ∠BGE = 40°.
∠AGE is vertically opposite ∠FGB, so ∠AGE = 140°.

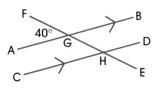

The pattern of angles around H is the same as that around G.
∠CHF corresponds to ∠AGF, so ∠CHF = 40°.
∠GHD corresponds to ∠FGB, so ∠GHD = 140°.
∠DHE corresponds to ∠BGE, so ∠DHE = 40°.
∠CHE corresponds to ∠AGE, so ∠CHE = 140°.

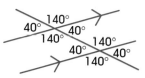

A

1. Calculate all the angles in each diagram. **Hint** Make a sketch of each diagram.

a

30°

b
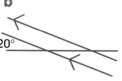
20°

c
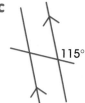
115°

d
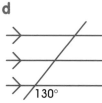
130°

2. Make a sketch of each diagram and write on it the size of each angle.

a   b   c   d

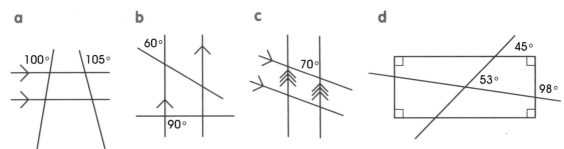

Hint The sides of a rectangle are parallel.

3. Below is a picture of the Leaning Tower of Pisa and a sketch showing some angles.

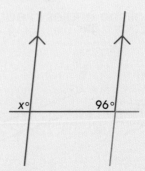

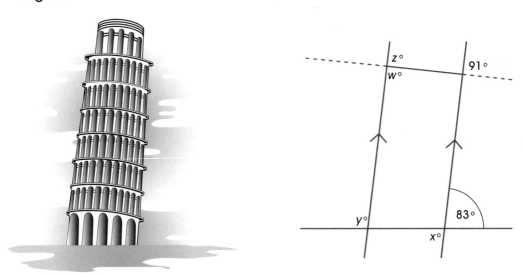

Calculate the size of:

a $x°$ b $y°$ c $z°$ d $w°$

giving a reason for each answer.

Adding Lines

Note that lines can be extended or added if it helps.

Example   Find x.

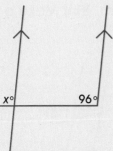

So we see that $x = 96$.

B

1. By copying the sketch and extending lines, find the labelled angles:

a

$100°$

$x°$

b

$y°$

$85°$

c

$25°$

$z°$

d

$a°$

$99°$

Any zig-zag formed by parallel lines can be adjusted in this manner.

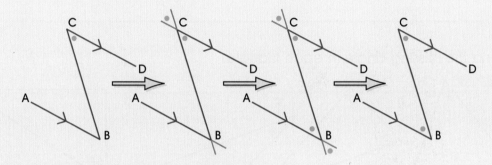

The angles 'inside the zig-zag' are equal.
We call such angles alternate angles.
$\angle ABC = \angle BCD$
They are alternate angles.

2. Name the alternate angles in each diagram.

a

Q   M

P   N

b

G

D

F

E

c

K   M

J

L

I

H

d

A ——— B
          >——C

D———
     E >— F

Hint There are 2 pairs.

3. Use alternate angles to help you find the labelled angles.

a

Q   M

$28°$ $p°$

P   N

b

 G

D

$36°$

F

$g°$

E

c

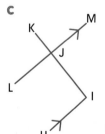

K   M

$i°$

$h°$

L

$92°$ I

H

d

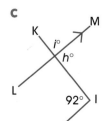

A ——— B
     $99°$ >——C

D———
  $n°$ $m°$
     E >— F

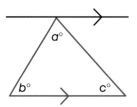

5 ▶ Angles in a Triangle

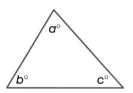
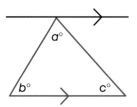
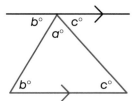
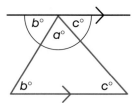

Draw any triangle angles $a°$, $b°$ and $c°$.

Draw a line parallel to the base.

Mark equal angles (alternate angles).

Note that $a° + b° + c°$ make a straight line.

The angles of a triangle add up to 180°.

A

1. Find the missing angle in each triangle.

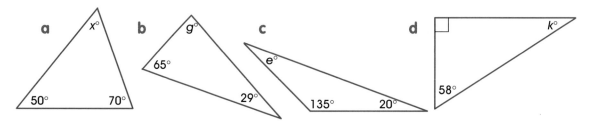

a $x°$, $50°$, $70°$

b $g°$, $65°$, $29°$

c $e°$, $135°$, $20°$

d $k°$, $58°$

2. The sails of a yacht are triangular as shown.

   a Calculate the size of the angle marked d.
   b What is the value of q?

3. ABCD is a rectangle representing a flag.
   $\angle ADB = 26°$

   a What is the size of $\angle DAC$?
      Give a reason.
   b What is the size of $\angle AED$?
   c Sketch the rectangle and fill in the sizes of all the angles.

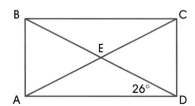

4. In the diagram, SR is parallel to PQ.
∠PQS = 28°
∠SRP = 35°

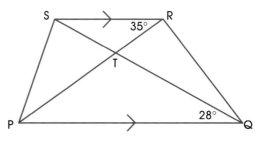

   a What is the size of ∠RPQ?
   b Calculate the size of ∠PTQ.
   c Copy the diagram and find the size
      of as many angles as you can.

   Hint You can't find them all!

5. A wooden framework is triangular and symmetrical.

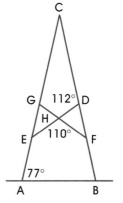

   a ∠CAB = 77°
      What is the size of ∠CBA?
   b Now calculate the size of ∠ACB.
   c ∠CDE = 112°
      By looking at triangle CDE,
      calculate the size of ∠CED.
   d ∠EHF = 110°
      What is the size of ∠DHF?
   e State the sizes of the three angles in triangle GHE.

Investigate

Draw two lines that are parallel.
Draw several transversals (shown in black).
Measure the pairs of angles trapped between
the lines and each transversal.
Find the sums of a + b, c + d and e + f.

What do you notice?

Can you explain what is happening?

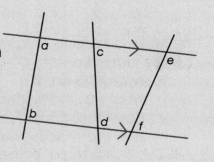

Unit 3 Information Handling

The Census is a giant snapshot of the whole nation

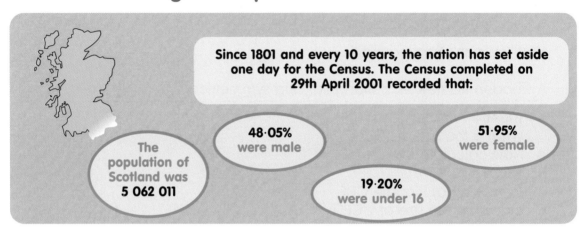

Since 1801 and every 10 years, the nation has set aside one day for the Census. The Census completed on 29th April 2001 recorded that:

The population of Scotland was **5 062 011**

48·05% were male

19·20% were under 16

51·95% were female

1 Looking Back

1. These are the house numbers of Primary 7 pupils

   26   3   41   55   200   19   11   7   67   103   16   8   40
   53   15   12   17   188   42   17   30   5   83   121   22   73

   a   Make a table to organise this data.
   Use class intervals of 1–50, 51–100, 101–150, 151–200 and 201–250
   to record the data.
   b   i   What was the highest house number recorded?
       ii   How many house numbers were larger than 50 but smaller than 100?
       iii   How many house numbers were larger than 100?

2. Pupils design a questionnaire to find out about computer use.
   This is an example of a completed form:

1	Do you use the computer at home?	yes	✓	no						
2	If yes, how many hours a week?	less than 2		2 to 4		4 to 6	✓	6 to 8		more than 8	
3	What do you use it for?	games		Internet	✓	letters	✓	other			
4	Do you use the computer at work?	yes		no	✓						
5	If yes, how many hours a day?	less than 2		2 to 4		4 to 6		6 to 8		more than 8	

a i Does this person use the computer at home?
  ii For how many hours do they use it each week?
  iii What do they use it for?

b Why is there no tick in row 5?

3. The information gathered is summarised below:

1	Do you use the computer at home?	yes	27	no	15							
2	If yes, how many hours a week?	less than 2	5	2 to 4	10	4 to 6	8	6 to 8	2	more than 8	2
3	What do you use it for?	games	12	internet	18	letters	24	other	6		
4	Do you use the computer at work?	yes	21	no	21						
5	If yes, how many hours a day?	less than 2	1	2 to 4	2	4 to 6	6	6 to 8	10	more than 8	2

a How many people were surveyed?
b Did more people use computers at home or at work?
c What was the most frequent answer to: **i** question **2** **ii** question **5**?
d i Find the total frequency for question **3**.
  ii Explain why it is possible for this total to be more than the total number of people surveyed.

4. These are six records of a database about the content of breakfast cereals. The figures given are for one serving.

Name	Hot/cold	Calories	Protein (g)	Fat (g)	Carbohydrates (g)
Early Munch	Hot	120	8	5	21
Toasty Oats	Hot	107	5·2	5	25
Apple Crunch	Cold	124	4	6	19·5
Brekky Bran	Cold	75	3	3	18
Crispy Clusters	Cold	105	6	4	22
Fruity Flakes	Cold	110	7·5	4	31

There are two field types in the Cereals database: **text** and **number**.

a What type of field is:
  i the **Name** field? **ii** the **Protein** field?

b Sort the cereal names out according to calories, putting the one that contains the most calories first.

If you have access to a computer, create a database about breakfast cereals.

c   Open a **New Database** file.

d   Give your database three fields. Use the **Name** of cereal and choose two other table headings.

e   Enter the **field names**. Make sure the correct **field type** is selected as you create each field.

f   Enter the data for the first record, Early Munch.

g   Select a new blank record and continue adding the data about cereals until you have all six records in your database.

h   Sort the records by cereal name alphabetically.

   i   Which cereal is now listed first in the database?

   ii   Which cereal is now listed last in the database?

5.   The cost, per box, of each cereal is given below:

Brekky Bran £1·24	Early Munch £1·45
Toasty Oats £1·18	Fruity Flakes £1·24
Apple Crunch £2·10	Crispy Clusters £1·95

The school breakfast club buys 4 boxes of Early Munch and Fruity Flakes, 3 boxes of Crispy Clusters, 2 boxes of Brekky Bran and Toasty Oats and a box of Apple Crunch.

a   i   **If you have access to a computer**, create the following spreadsheet:

	A	B	C	D
1	Name of Cereal	No. of Boxes sold	Price per box	Total
2				
3				

   ii   Insert multiplication formulae in column D to calculate the total spent by the breakfast club on each type of cereal.
Remember A formula always starts with =
Example In D2 enter = **B2 *C2**

   iii   Insert an **Overall Total** label in cell C7.

   iv   Insert an adding formula in cell D7 to calculate the amount of money spent on the breakfast cereals altogether (= **D2 + D3 + D4 + D5 + D6**).

b If the cereal data is entered in the order given at the beginning of this question, what number will appear in cell   i C2   ii C4?

c What number will appear in cell   i D2   ii D4   iii D7?

d On which cereal was most money spent?

2   A Quest for Data

Some types of data can be found by searching in books or on the Internet. Other types of data have to be collected by direct observation and questioning.

A good questionnaire is an efficient way of collecting data.
When designing questionnaires, you must:

* think carefully about the type of data you want to collect
* give clear choices, for example **every day** is better than **often**
* keep questions simple
* try to get a **representative sample**.

1. Rewrite and improve each of the following questions.

    a How much chocolate do you eat?   i a little   ii a lot

    b Do you not enjoy going to see no nonsense movies?

    c Would you prefer to go out to the cinema or perhaps go ice-skating with a group of friends?

2. You are going to design a questionnaire to find out about reading habits.

    a Make decisions about your sample:
       i How many people will be asked?
       ii Does age matter?
       iii Where will you ask people?
       iv What time period will the survey cover (for example, every interval for a week)?

    b Design your questionnaire to gather data on these points:
       i Is reading enjoyed?
       ii How often do people read?
       iii What type of books are preferred?

3. Design a questionnaire to find out about journeys to school.

    a Decide on your representative sample.

    b Design your questionnaire to gather data on these points:
       i length of journey
       ii duration of journey
       iii method of transport

3 Investigating and Organising Information

A

1. Data is shown on the lengths of 13 Scottish bridges.

   a Copy the table below.
   b Complete the class interval column.
   c Enter the bridge names.
   d Complete the frequency column.

   Scalpay Bridge 300 m   Glenfinnan Viaduct 380 m
   Forth Bridge 2528 m   Clava Viaduct 549 m
   Tay Road Bridge 2253 m   Findhorn Viaduct 400 m
   North Bridge 346 m   Forth Road Bridge 1828 m
   Kessock Bridge 1052 m   Tay Railway Bridge 3135 m
   George IV Bridge 300 m   Erskine Bridge 660 m
   Skye Bridge 570 m

Length (m)	Frequency	Name of Bridge
1–500		
501–1000		

2. Four plants are measured as they grow over a period of a month.
   All four plants were 5 cm to start with.

   Plant 1 was watered and given lots of sunlight. After 1 month it measured 22 cm.

   Plant 2 was watered, given plant food, but no sunlight. After 1 month it measured 15 cm.

   Plant 3 was given lots of sunlight and plant food, but no water. It had dried out, died and measured 3 cm after 1 month.

   Plant 4 was given lots of sunlight, water and plant food. It measured 26 cm after 1 month.

   a Design a table to organise the plant data.
   b Add a row or column to your table to record the **Change in Height** over the month.
   c Which of the three factors, sunlight, plant food or water, seemed to be most important for the growth of the plants?

3. The results of the 50 m breaststroke have been recorded. The times are measured in seconds.

50 m breaststroke results							
Lane 1	Lane 2	Lane 3	Lane 4	Lane 5	Lane 6	Lane 7	Lane 8
40·25	40·05	41·18	40·88	41·15	39·69	43·03	41·31

a Design a table to sort the lane numbers by time (fastest to slowest).
b This race was a heat. To qualify for the next round, swimmers had to swim faster than forty and a half seconds. How many swimmers qualified?

◆ Investigate

A Statistical Investigation

a What is the most common number of pages in a unit of this book?
  i Design a tally chart to record your findings.
  ii Draw a suitable graph to display the data from your tally chart and use your chart and graph to help you answer the question.

b Does the first unit of the book have more questions per page than the last unit?
c Do the even numbered pages of the book have more pictures than the odd?

◇ B

1. The speed that a person responds or reacts to something is called his or her reaction time.

An experiment was done to measure the reactions of pupils in a Primary 7 class. Pupils took it in turns to rest one wrist on a desk. Without warning, a ruler was allowed to drop between the pupil's thumb and forefinger. The pupil had to grasp the ruler as quickly as possible. The length of ruler that has fallen is a measure of his reaction time.

The data given are measurements in centimetres.

7	9	11·5	6	7	9	9·5	10
6·5	5	12	5·5	5	8	8·5	7
9	6	5·5	6	7·5	5	6·5	10

Measurement (cm)	Tally	Count

a Copy the table and complete the **Measurement (cm)** column.
Note that there are only four rows – you will need to decide on suitable groupings for the data.

b Enter the data into the table.

 # 4 Organising Data – Spreadsheets

A spreadsheet will calculate when a Formula is entered in a cell.
A formula must start with an = sign.
Mathematical symbols are used in formulae to instruct the spreadsheet to perform many different mathematical operations.

+ add   − subtract   * multiply   / divide

	A	B	C
1	24	34	=A1+B1
2	54	87	
3	72	15	

	A	B	C
1	24	34	58
2	54	87	
3	72	15	

        Type this . . .   . . . get this.

A label, number or formula can quickly be copied into other cells using the Fill shortcut.

	A	B	C
1	24	34	=A1+B1
2	54	87	
3	72	15	

	A	B	C
1	24	34	=A1+B1
2	54	87	=A2+B2
3	72	15	=A3+B3

    Highlight C1, C2 and C3   . . . Fill down to get . . .

Note This puts *similar* formulae into cells C2 and C3 and not the same formula.

1. Some pupils are going on an adventure break to Craggy Hills Outdoor Centre. The cost of the break is £95·00. The teacher has been recording the money collected, over the last 8 weeks.

Week 1	
Jane	£15
Tina	£7·50
Lee	£12
Jim	£16
Jake	£25

Week 2	
Lynn	£16·50
Jim	£10
Lee	£12
Alan	£20
Jane	£15

Week 3	
Colin	£32
Jake	£25
Lee	£12
Jane	£15
Lynn	£18·50

Week 4	
Tina	£7·50
Lee	£12
Jane	£15
Lynn	£12·50
Peter	£95

Week 5	
Jake	£25
Lee	£12
Jim	£20
Lynn	£10·50
Tina	£7·50

Week 6	
Jane	£15
Lee	£12
Jim	£16
Lynn	£12·50
Colin	£32

Week 7	
Jane	£15
Lee	£12
Jake	£20
Lynn	£12·50
Colin	£31

Week 8	
Jane	£5
Lee	£11
Jim	£16
Lynn	£12·00
Alan	£50

a Make a table to keep a record of the payments.

If you have access to a computer make a copy of the spreadsheet below and complete it.

	A	B	C	D	E	F	G	H	I	J	K
1	Name	Week 1	Week 2	Week 3	Week 4	Week 5	Week 6	Week 7	Week 8	Total	Still to pay
2	Jane	£ 15.00	£ 15.00							£ 30.00	£ 65.00
3	Tina	£ 7.50								£ 7.50	£ 87.50
4	Lee	£ 12.00	£ 12.00							£ 24.00	£ 71.00
5	Jim	£ 16.00	£ 10.00							£ 26.00	£ 69.00
6	Jake	£ 25.00								£ 25.00	£ 70.00
7	Lynn		£ 16.50							£ 16.50	£ 78.50
8	Alan		£ 20.00							£ 20.00	£ 75.00
9	Colin									£ 0.00	£ 95.00
10	Peter									£ 0.00	£ 95.00

Note

✤ All the cells that will hold money data have been formatted for currency. To do this, select **Cells** (Excel) or **Number** (AppleWorks) from the **Format** menu, then select **Currency** and **2 decimal places**.

✤ J2 holds a formula that adds the cells B2 to I2.

✤ K2 holds a formula that subtracts the contents of J2 from £95·00.

✤ J2 and K2 are filled down to row 10.

b   Make a list of the pupils sorted by how much they still have to pay after 8 weeks.

*If you are working at a computer, this can be done by asking the spreadsheet to **Sort**.*

c   On which week was most money gathered?

d   How much money has been paid in altogether over the 8 weeks?

Put a formula in J11 to sum J2 to J10.

e   How much money has still to be gathered, so that all pupils have paid in full?

Put a formula in K11 to sum K2 to K10.

2.   The data below lists the national record times for men's flat racing before the 1984 Olympics. The times are recorded in seconds.

Australia		France		USA		United Kingdom	
100 m	10·31	100 m	10·11	100 m	9·93	100 m	10·11
200 m	20·06	200 m	20·38	200 m	19·75	200 m	20·21
400 m	44·84	400 m	45·28	400 m	43·86	400 m	44·93
800 m	104·40	800 m	103·80	800 m	103·80	800 m	102·00
1500 m	214·20	1500 m	214·20	1500 m	211·80	1500 m	210·60
5000 m	796·80	5000 m	800·40	5000 m	792·00	5000 m	780·60
10 000 m	1659·60	10 000 m	1678·20	10 000 m	1645·80	10 000 m	1650·60

a   Make a table that organises the data in a better manner.
Use five columns headed: **Distance, Australia, France, USA, UK**.

If you have access to a computer then make a spreadsheet.
Note that the units are mentioned in the heading rather than with the numbers. This way, the spreadsheet will allow the numbers to be used in formulae.

	A	B
1	Distance (m)	Australia (sec)
2	100	10.31
3	200	20.06
4	400	44.84
5	800	104.4
6	1500	214.2
7	5000	796.8
8	10 000	1659.6
9	10 000 (min)	27.66

b Convert the times for the 10 000 m into minutes.

On the computer, to do this for Australia enter = B8/60

c Create a **Fastest Country** column.

Scan the four results for each event to find the country with the fastest time. Record the country's name in the appropriate cell. Try this in F2: =MIN(B2..E2). It will come up with the smallest value in these cells.

3. The data below describes World Record times for various distances in 2004. The data are: name of event, time (seconds), name of athlete, athlete's country, date of record, location where record was achieved.

100 m	200 m	400 m	800 m	1500 m	5000 m	10 000 m
9·78	19·32	43·18	101·11	206·00	759·36	1582·75
Tim Montgomery	Michael Johnson	Michael Johnson	Wilson Kipketer	Hicham El Guerrouj	Haile Gebrselassie	Haile Gebrselassie
USA	USA	USA	Denmark	Morocco	Ethiopia	Ethiopia
14 Sep 2002	01 Aug 1996	26 Aug 1999	24 Jul 1997	14 Jul 1998	13 Jun 1998	01 Jun 1998
Paris	Atlanta	Seville	Cologne	Rome	Helsinki	Hengelo

a Make a table to organise the data better.

If you are making a spreadsheet, remember to put all units in the headings.

b Express all the times in minutes correct to two decimal places.

If you are using a spreadsheet, add a column with a formula for dividing the seconds by 60.

c The 100 m, 200 m and 400 m World Record times above are held by Americans.

  i Enter the heading **Decrease in 1984 USA Record** in a new column.
  ii Use the USA 100 m, 200 m and 400 m record information from question **2** to help you work out how much the old record has been beaten by.

Use **Subtraction Formulae** if you are working with a spreadsheet.

5 Organising Data – Databases

Vast amounts of data can be stored, sorted, searched and viewed using a **computer database**. There are different types of fields, each handled differently by the computer.

For example, **text** field, **number** field, **date** field, **time** field.

A

1. Look back at the data given on World Record times in question **3** of the previous exercise. If a database has been created using this data:

   a Name the fields making up the database.

   b Three field types would make up the database: number, text and date. The **Event** field will be a number field and typed as **Event (m)**.

      i What does the **m** represent?

      ii Why must the **m** be added to the field name and not typed with the record data?

   c If you have access to a computer, create a database about the World Record times.

   d Open a **New Database** file.

   e Define the **fields**. Make sure the correct **field type** is selected as you create each field.

   f Enter the data for the first record: Data about Tim Montgomery.

   g Select a new blank record and continue adding the record data until you have all seven records in your database.

   h Sort the records by date in ascending order.

      i Which record has stood the longest?

      ii Which record was most recently set?

   i Search the records for the athlete Haile Gebrselassie.

      i How many of the records stored did he set?

      ii Where did he set these records?

◆ Investigate

Search in books or on the Internet for information about World Record times. Check whether the records in your database have been broken. Add more records to your database. You could collect female records as well or different male events.

In 1876, Melvil Dewey, an American librarian, invented a way of arranging non-fiction library books to make them easier to find. This system is known as the Dewey Decimal Classification System and is used in many libraries all over the world today.

Dewey's system categorises books into main areas which are subdivided and subdivided again using decimals.

Example
700	The Arts
790	Recreational and Performing Arts
797	Aquatic and Air Sports
797·12	Boating
797·122	Canoeing

 ## Looking Back

1. Here is a number line. The small un-numbered marks represent **hundredths** (0·01).

Arrow a points to 0·01.
To what numbers are the other arrows pointing?
Write your answers in decimal form.

2. In the number 15·97, the red digit stands for 9 tenths or 0·9.
Write down the value of the red digit in the following numbers:

    a 23·6   b 345·8   c 78·87   d 670·3   e 800·3   f 90·09

3. Write out each list in order, smallest first:

a 10·3	19	13·7	1·9	0·8	6·2
b 72·6 kg	64·8 kg	72·0 kg	59·3 kg	70 kg	65·5 kg
c 12·07 m	80·8 m	3·07 m	44·04 m	80·82 m	44·4 m
d £27·30	£0·45	£18	£27·03	£1·45	£16·99

4. Add or subtract these numbers mentally:

   a 140 + 250   b 500 + 400   c 330 − 110
   d 900 − 300   e 230 + 150   f 560 − 240

5. Two taxi drivers compared the amount of petrol they used during their weekend shifts. Pat used 73·9 litres and Davy used 85·3 litres.

   a What was the total volume of petrol used by the two drivers?
   b How many more litres did Davy use than Pat?

6. At a Lego exhibition, a model of Edinburgh Castle weighed 90·3 kg.
   A model of Tower Bridge weighed 11·7 kg less.
   What was the weight of the Tower Bridge model?

7. Kasim bought a new pair of jeans for £44·49.
   His friend Chris bought a pair for £39·99.

   a How much did they spend altogether?
   b Calculate the difference in the cost of Chris and Kasim's jeans.

8. The Docherty family drove from their home in Largs to visit friends in Falkirk. They stopped for a break in Paisley before continuing their journey.

   a Calculate the total distance of their journey.
   b How much further is the drive from Paisley to Falkirk than the drive from Largs to Paisley?

56·64 km

Falkirk

36·48 km

Paisley

Largs

9. Hartz Rent-a-Car offer a variety of different cars to hire.

   a How much more per day does it cost to hire the Locus than the Siesta?
   b The cost of hiring a Jeep for the day costs £8·79 more than the cost of the Locus.

   How much does it cost to hire the Jeep?

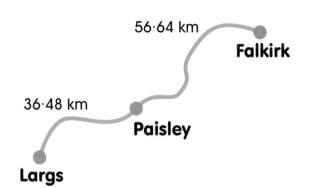

Locus
£32·25 per day

Siesta
£24·49 per day

2 Thousandths

A

1. Write the following in decimal form:

   a 3 thousandths   b 8 thousandths   c 5 thousandths
   d 15 thousandths   e 67 thousandths   f 139 thousandths
   g 322 thousandths   h 500 thousandths

2. In this number line, the small un-numbered marks represent thousandths (0·001).

   Arrow **a** points to 0·252.
   To what numbers are the other arrows pointing?
   Write your answers in decimal form.

3. Make a copy of this number line.

   ```
   0·48         0·49         0·50         0·51
   ```

   a Draw arrows to show the position of:
      i 0·491   ii 0·487   iii 0·505   iv 0·511   v 0·483

   b Use your arrows to help you write the numbers in order, smallest first.

4. Write each of the following lists in order, smallest first.

   a 0·234   0·321   0·014   0·108   0·022   0·313
   b 0·081   1·018   5·201   0·007   0·700   3·323
   c 1·234 m   0·235 m   5·005 m   0·808 m   2·003 m   0·444 m
   d 6·602 g   0·62 g   0·602 g   6·002 g   6·202 g   2·206 g

5. Copy and complete each of the following sequences.

   a 0·001   0·002   0·003   —   —   —
   b 0·029   0·031   0·033   —   —   —
   c 2·225   2·230   2·235   —   —   —
   d 5·012   5·011   5·010   —   —   —
   e 1·150 kg   1·200 kg   1·250 kg   —   —   —
   f 4·915 km   4·910 km   4·905 km   —   —   —

6. Kieran picked the five tiles shown below and arranged them to make the largest possible number he could with 3 decimal places.

| 7 | · | 5 | 2 | 1 |

a Arrange these tiles to make numbers to 3 decimal places. Make:
   i the smallest possible number
   ii the number nearest to the value 6.

b Lisa picked four different digits and the decimal point tile.

| · | 0 | 9 | 3 | 8 |

Arrange these tiles to make numbers to 3 decimal places. Make:
   i the largest possible number
   ii the smallest possible number
   iii the number nearest to the value 1.

3 ▶ Adding

◆ A ◆

1. Add the following pairs of numbers:

   a 37·3 + 29·65 b 55·36 + 39·7 c 46 + 28·19 d 136 + 84·3
   e 22·56 + 59   f 75·24 + 19·9 g 193 + 76·8   h 39·9 + 39·99
   i 28 + 67·68   j 97·8 + 195

2. Calculate:

   a 13·56 + 19·2 + 17·6   b 29·8 + 0·99 + 36·6
   c 71·2 + 8·34 + 2·58   d 55·37 + 9·45 + 16·6
   e 48 + 15·8 + 23·5   f 15·65 + 34·26 + 8
   g 23·42 + 25 + 26·8   h 60·28 + 13·7 + 22·5

3. Add the following pairs of decimals **mentally**:

   a 7·3 + 7·1   b 4·4 + 8·6   c 5·5 + 5·4   d 3·4 + 9·5
   e 8·7 + 7·2   f 6·2 + 6·8   g 11·4 + 6·5   h 15·1 + 3·7
   i 13·6 + 6·3   j 15·6 + 7·1   k 18·3 + 8·5   l 17·2 + 12·8

4. At 9 a.m. the temperature in Primary 7's classroom was 14·7°C.
   By 12 noon this had risen by a further 7·8°C.
   What was the temperature at 12 noon?

5. Fiona bought a new pair of trainers in a sports sale, saving £8·99.
   If she paid £54·75, what was the original cost of the trainers?

6. At a carpet store, Jean spotted a roll of carpet that she liked.
   But it was 12·49 m in length – 2·87 m shorter than she needed.
   What length of carpet was Jean looking for?

7. The pop group *New Addition* were playing in concert at the exhibition centre.
   Michael travelled a distance of 23·78 km to get there.
   Gary travelled 19·34 km.

   a What was the total distance travelled by Michael and Gary?
   b Laura travelled 8·7 km further than the total travelled by Michael and Gary. What distance did Laura travel?
   c A variety of band merchandise was on sale.
   Laura spent £28 on two items.
   What did she buy?
   d Gary spent £34·50 on three items.
   What did he buy?
   e Michael just bought a CD. How much did the three of them spend altogether?

Band Merchandise

T-Shirt **£9·40**
Cap **£8·55**
CD **£15**
Poster **£5·65**
Sweatshirt **£19·45**
Signed photo **£12**

Challenge

Which three of these numbers add up to 50?

| 17·4 | 18·7 | 16·54 | 14·43 | 18·27 | 14·33 |

 B

1. Calculate (Remember to add trailing zeros if needed):

   a 4·28 + 3·819   b 6·278 + 0·98   c 4·964 + 3·85
   d 7·967 + 1·64   e 5·9 + 3·803   f 4·7 + 1·345 + 3·38
   g 5 + 3·77 + 0·648 h 3·7 + 2 + 1·558

2. Add the following decimals **mentally**:

a 12·3 + 13·6	b 15·3 + 9·7	c 28·7 + 8·2
d 44·2 + 8·7	e 15·4 + 17·5	f 26·1 + 15·7
g 5·2 + 7·1 + 8·3	h 12·3 + 2·5 + 8·2	i 9·2 + 9·3 + 9·4
j 9·9 + 8·7	k 16·5 + 7·6	l 14·3 + 14·8

3. In the standing long jump competition, Tracey's three attempts were:

> 0·786 m   1·36 m   1·093 m

   a What was the combined total of her attempts?
   b The winner jumped 0·657 m more than Tracey's best attempt.
     How far did the winner jump?

4. Aisha took three parcels to the Post Office.
   Parcel A weighed 1·78 kg
   Parcel B weighed 3·655 kg
   Parcel C weighed 2·39 kg more than the combined weight of A and B.
   What is the weight of Parcel C?

5. Which three of these bottles of soft drink have a
   combined volume of 10 litres?

Challenge

Kelly was using a blotchy pen.
Can you work out which digits have been covered by the blots?

a
```
  4 ✱ 3 7
+ 2·5 ✱ 7
─────────
  6·7 0 ✱
```

b
```
  1·7 ✱ 9
+ 5·✱ 8 4
─────────
  ✱·1 1 ✱
```

c
```
  ✱·3 ✱ 7
+ 5·✱ 9 ✱
─────────
  8·7 6 2
```

d
```
  ✱·9 ✱ ✱
+ 0·✱ 7 6
─────────
  8·8 3 0
```

Subtracting

A

1. Calculate:

a	33·2 − 17·18	b	40·5 − 27·27	c	55·2 − 12·85	d	70·1 − 9·75
e	180 − 18·8	f	37 − 13·48	g	123 − 25·7	h	60 − 38·43

2. Subtract the following decimals **mentally**:

a	8·8 − 2·3	b	7·6 − 3·1	c	11·8 − 3·5	d	15·5 − 5·1
e	19·9 − 10·7	f	16·6 − 7·1	g	20·5 − 5·5	h	21·7 − 11·6
i	22·4 − 7·3	j	20·7 − 11·7	k	25·4 − 9·3	l	30·7 − 15·3

3. The length of an NBA basketball court is 28·7 m.
   Dribbleford Primary's court has a length of 23·95 m.
   How much longer is the length of the NBA court?

4. For the parent's coffee morning two urns were used.
   Urn A held 30 litres of water.
   Urn B held 35·7 litres of water.

   a By 11 a.m., 12·9 litres had been used from Urn A
   and 16·25 litres from Urn B.
   How much water still remained in each urn?
   b By 11·30 a.m., a further 8·76 litres had been used from Urn A
   and 9·99 litres from Urn B.
   i Which urn had the most water left in it? ii How much more?

5. Four friends compared how much money they had saved for their
   holidays.

   Jackie £28·19   Geoff £30·16   George £39·71   Lydia £34·21

   a Calculate the difference between the largest and smallest amounts
   saved.
   b Lydia had hoped to save £50. How much was she short of her target?
   c How much more money did George and Lydia save together than
   Geoff and Jackie?

> **Challenge**
>
> Choose four numbers from the box to complete the calculations.
>
>
>
> 13·65 13·45
> 16·75 15·44
> 14·24 15·25
>
> 75·1 − ☐ − ☐ = 46·2
>
> 41·44 − ☐ − 13·75 = ☐

1. Calculate, remembering to add trailing zeros where required:

   a 7·27 − 3·186   b 9·05 − 2·349   c 5·22 − 2·738   d 6·11 − 3·373
   e 8·1 − 5·468   f 3·7 − 1·888   g 9 − 2·139   h 4 − 1·758

2. Subtract the following decimals **mentally**:

   a 10·8 − 3·5   b 17·3 − 9·2   c 30·6 − 17·3   d 23·6 − 15·5
   e 40·7 − 18·5   f 32·4 − 17·2   g 41·7 − 14·7   h 53·8 − 14·6
   i 38·5 − 18·1   j 42·9 − 14·7   k 20 − 8·3   l 40 − 11·3

3. Karen often cycles to her friend's house. She can go one way, cycling a distance of 3·1 km, or take a short cut and cycle 2·398 km.
   Calculate the difference between the cycling routes.

4. Sammy's Smoothies are sold in 1·755 litre and 2·49 litre bottles.
   What is the difference in the volume of the two bottles?

5. Sweets are sold wholesale in jars of different weights.
   Calculate the difference in the weight of:

   a a jar of chocolate limes and cola cubes
   b a jar of sherbet lemons and chocolate limes
   c a jar of cola cubes and sherbet lemons.

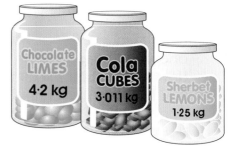

6. Iain was allowed to take hand luggage weighing up to 9 kg on board an aeroplane. His bag weighed 2·456 kg less than the limit.
   What was the weight of Iain's bag?

7. Mrs Blair compared the unit costs of three electrical companies.

   Calculate the difference in the cost between:

   a Sparks and Radiate for the first 100 units
   b Brite a Lite and Sparks for 100+ units.

	First 100 units	100+ units
Sparks	3·341p	2·9p
Brite a Lite	2·996p	1·776p
Radiate	4·2p	2·78p

Unit 5 — Time and Temperature

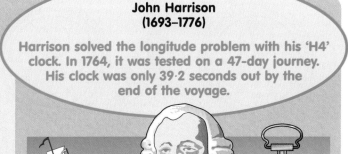

John Harrison (1693–1776)

Harrison solved the longitude problem with his 'H4' clock. In 1764, it was tested on a 47-day journey. His clock was only 39·2 seconds out by the end of the voyage.

Navigators in the 18th century found it difficult to know their position in the open sea. They could work out their latitude (north/south position) from the Pole Star. But to work out their longitude (east/west position) they had to use the position of the sun and the exact time. Clocks at that time just weren't accurate enough.

1 Looking Back

To find the gap between 4 minutes 40 seconds and 9 minutes 21 seconds:

min	sec		min	sec
9	21	→	8	81
4	40		4	40

Can't take 40 sec from 21 sec.

4 min 41 sec

1. a Write down the reading on this stopwatch.
    b What was the reading 2 minutes 55 seconds previously?
    c How long before it reads $9\frac{3}{4}$ minutes?

2. These stopwatches show the times of runners in a race:

Amy   Aileen   Asha

Alison   Anne

a Put the runners in order 1st, 2nd, 3rd, 4th and 5th.
b What was the gap in seconds between the winner and the last to finish?
c How many seconds did Anne take to run the race?

3. a Write down the temperature reading on each of these thermometers:

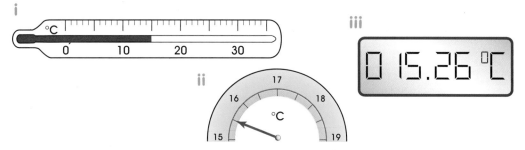

i

°C   0   10   20   30

iii

0 15.26 °C

ii

15   16   17   18   19
°C

b What is the lowest reading?
c Calculate the difference between the highest and lowest reading.

2 Measuring Time

Stopwatches and timers are used to measure the time gap between events. Some are more accurate than others. Scientists often need to use very accurate timing devices.

3.29.38 88
hours min   sec 1/100

More recent electronic timers can be accurate to $\frac{1}{100}$ sec (or better).

This shows a time of 3 hours 29 minutes 38·88 seconds

1. Say how accurate each of these timers is:

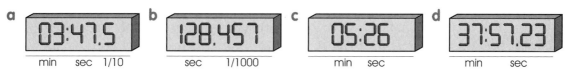

a 03:47.5   min sec 1/10
b 128.457   sec 1/1000
c 05:26   min sec
d 37:57.23   min sec

2. Convert each time shown to a decimal number of seconds, for example, 23·72 seconds:

a 02:08.2   min sec 1/10
b 04:15.26   min sec 1/100
c 01:00.2339   min sec 1/10 000

3. Write down each reading approximately to the nearest:
   i $\frac{1}{10}$ second   ii second   iii minute.

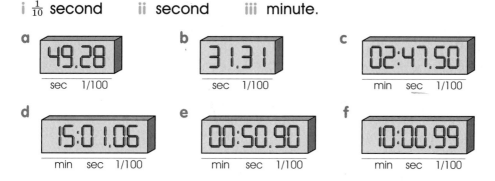

a 49.28   sec 1/100
b 31.31   sec 1/100
c 02:47.50   min sec 1/100
d 15:01.06   min sec 1/100
e 00:50.90   min sec 1/100
f 10:00.99   min sec 1/100

4. Use the headings: **min**, **sec** and **1/100** to write a timer display for these times:

   a 2 minutes 24 seconds   b 5 minutes 18·6 seconds
   c 12 minutes 49·03 seconds

5. For each timer display give the time:

   i 25·5 seconds earlier   ii 1 minute 45·6 seconds later.

a 01:06.2   min sec 1/10
b 09:21.05   min sec 1/100
c 02:14.43   min sec 1/100

6. Ailsa attempted to judge a time gap of one minute.
   She did this by saying: '1 thousand, 2 thousand, 3 thousand . . .' up to '60 thousand'. The timer recorded **00:59·40**.

   On average, how long, in seconds, did it take her to say each of the 60 phrases?

◆ Investigate

Timing Notes

The sound made by hitting a tuning fork creates waves in the air. The repeat of one wave is called a **cycle**. For example, middle C has 261·63 cycles each second. Thus it has a **frequency** of 261·63 cycles per second (c/s).

a Record the time for one cycle of a middle C note using this type of timer display:

b Here are the frequencies of some other notes:

sec   1/1000

Note	Frequency (c/s)
D	293·66
E	329·63
F	349·23
G	392·00
A	440·00

For each note, calculate the time for one cycle and record it as a timer display to **the nearest $\frac{1}{1000}$ sec**.

c Is this accuracy of timer suitable to tell the notes apart?

d Investigate whether this timer display would be accurate enough to tell the notes apart:

sec   1/10 000

3 Calculating Time

 A

1. Add each set of times:

   a   4 h 36 min and 1 h 47 min   b   43 min and 2 h 35 min
   c   45 min 26 s and 43 min 29 s   d   3h 21 min 55 s and 2 h 38 min 5 s

2. Find the difference between the shortest and longest of the four times in each part of Question **1** above.

3. Calculate:

   a   45 min × 5   b   1 h 26 min × 4   c   2 h 10 min 23 s × 3
   d   7 h 30 min ÷ 6   e   2 h 21 min 10 s ÷ 7   f   13 h ÷ 8

4. A CD of Mendelssohn's music uses the notation 12'36 to mean a track
   lasting 12 minutes 36 seconds.
   There are nine tracks in total listed with playing times:
   22'02, 3'27, 2'17, 1'36, 1'08, 2'44, 1'10, 2'20 and 6'46

   a   Is the first track longer than all the other tracks put
        together? Show your calculations.
   b   Divide the total length of the tracks by the number
        of tracks to calculate the mean length of a track.

5. Each day Mairi's mum does a 3 min 45 s yoga exercise.

   a   How long does she spend each week doing yoga?
   b   How long did she spend doing yoga during
        September?

6. Peter delivers eight newspapers, taking him 1 h 12 min.

   a   On average how long is this for each newspaper?
   b   If he took 15 seconds less, on average, to deliver
        each newspaper, how long would his deliveries take?

7. Martha is downloading small pictures from the Internet.
   Each picture takes 48 seconds to download.

   a   How long will it take to download 15 pictures?
   b   In the same time she could download five big pictures.
        How long does each big picture take to download?
   c   Another collection contains eight small and seven big pictures.
        How long should this collection take to download?

8. The average time taken to cut down a small Norway Spruce tree in Mabie
   Forest is 6 min 30 s. Larger trees take an average of 7 min 27 s.

   a   Approximately how many small trees can be cut down in an hour?
   b   Approximately how many larger trees can be cut down in an hour?
   c   A tree feller cuts down 10 small and 20 large trees. He starts work at
        9.00 a.m. and takes two 15-minute breaks. When does he finish?

Challenge

Decimal Memory Madness

When you divide the distance around a circle by the distance across a circle, you always get the same answer no matter the size of the circle. Mathematicians call this number **Pi**. It is a number starting 3·1415926 . . . and going on forever.

Hideaki Tomoyori from Yokohama in Japan recited Pi from memory to 40 000 decimal places in 17 h 21 min. This included breaks totalling 4 h 15 min and took place in 1987.

a   How long would it have taken him without breaks?
b   How long would 10 000 places have taken with no breaks?
c   If he had recited 1 million places with no breaks,
    how long would it have taken?

Investigate

Calculator Secrets

Calculators often have one of these two keys:
What do these keys do? Investigate!   o ' '' | D M S

Hint What is 3 h 25 min + 2 h 50 m?   Try 3 [DMS] 25 + 2 [DMS] 50 =

4 Below Zero

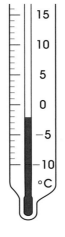

The thermometer is
showing a temperature
of −2°C

Minus two degrees

−2 is a negative number

Negative two

Above freezing:

positive temperatures

Freezing point is 0° Celsius

Below freezing:

negative temperatures

A

1. Make a larger version of the scale on this thermometer and mark in arrows showing:

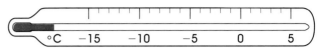

a 2°C   b −2°C   c −4°C   d −12°C

2. Write down the temperatures shown by the arrows:

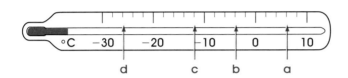

3. Write down the temperature shown on each thermometer:

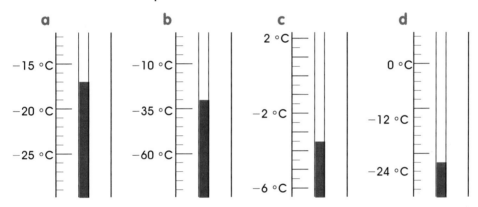

4. a Sort these temperatures into increasing order: 4°C, −3°C, −8°C, 2°C, 0°C, −18°C

   b Sort these temperatures into decreasing order: −5°C, −2°C, 2°C, 5°C, −15°C, −14°C

5. a How many degrees warmer is Frankfurt than:

   i Belgrade   ii Helsinki   iii Chicago?

   b How many degrees colder is Chicago than:

   i Helsinki   ii Belgrade   iii Frankfurt?

   c Give the temperature of each town if its temperature:

   i increases by 3°C   ii decreases by 2°C.

Belgrade:	−2°C
Chicago:	−12°C
Frankfurt:	1°C
Helsinki:	−8°C

B

1. Write down the temperatures shown on these dials:

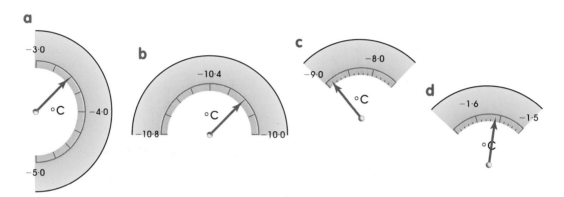

a

b

c

d

2. Here is a table of lowest recorded temperatures:

a Which location had:
   i the lowest
   ii the highest
      temperature?

b For each location
   calculate the
   difference between
   the lowest and
   highest temperature.

Location	Lowest	Highest
Africa	−23·9°C (Morocco)	57·7°C (Libya)
Antarctica	−89·2°C (Vostock)	14·6°C (Hope Bay)
Australia	−23·0°C (Charlotte Ross)	50·7°C (Oodnadatta)
Europe	−55·0°C (Russia)	50·0°C (Spain)
North America	−63·0°C (Canada)	56·7°C (Death Valley, USA)

3. When gases are cooled they become a liquid.
   This temperature is called the boiling point.
   Here are some gases and their boiling points:

a Write the gases in order of increasing
   boiling point.

b A mixture of all the gases is cooled.
   In what order will the gases change to
   liquid?

c The lowest temperature possible is
   −273·2°C (**absolute zero**).
   For each gas calculate the difference
   between its boiling point and absolute zero.

Gas	Boiling Point
Hydrogen	−252·9°C
Helium	−268·6°C
Oxygen	−183·0°C
Nitrogen	−195·8°C
Neon	−246·1°C

Unit 6 Position and Movement

This picture shows one of the early maps of the world constructed by Claudius Ptolemaeus, or Ptolemy, in about **150 AD**

Today we refer to maps to find out our current position and identify where we want to go

For a long time people have used maps to find their way around. **Cartography** is the science of making maps. The oldest known maps were created on clay tablets by the Babylonians around 2300 BC.

1 Looking Back

1. A group of people went for a walk on the Isle of Arran.

   a i Charles was facing south and turned 45° clockwise.

   ii Seona was facing north-east and turned 90° clockwise.

   iii Jean was facing south-west and turned 90° anticlockwise.

   Write down the new direction each person was facing.

   b i Tariq turned from east to south-west clockwise.

   ii Rachel turned from north-west to south-east anticlockwise.

   Write the size of the angles through which these walkers turned.

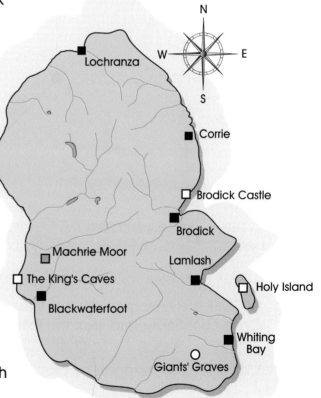

2. To travel from Blackwaterfoot to Machrie Moor, the walkers must go north.
    In which direction do they travel going from:

    a   Holy Island to The King's Caves
    b   Whiting Bay to Machrie Moor
    c   Lochranza to Corrie
    d   Lamlash to Giants' Graves
    e   Brodick to Machrie Moor?

3. Travelling east (E) you are on a bearing of 090°.
    What is your bearing when you are travelling:

    a S   b N   c SE   d NE   e W   f SW   g NW?
    Remember Every direction is represented by a 3-digit number.

4. The bearing of the yacht from the lighthouse L is 070°.
    Use a protractor to measure the bearing of each yacht from L.

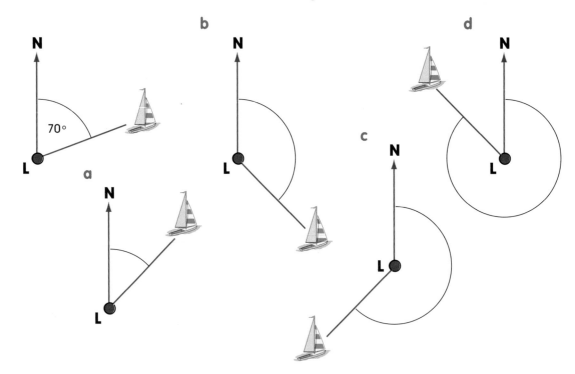

5. ABCDEF is a hexagon with two lines of symmetry.
    On a coordinate grid, plot the following points:
    A (5,2)   B (3,2)   C (2,4)   D (3,6)   E (5,6)
    Complete the hexagon by plotting point F and write down its coordinates.

6. a   PQRS is a quadrilateral with these vertices:
        P (0,4)   Q (0,8)   R (4,8)   S (6,2)
        Identify the type of quadrilateral.

    b   At which point do its diagonals intersect?

7. Guide the mouse through the coordinate grid to the cheese, staying on the gridlines. Write down the route.

   Hint Begin with (1, 0), (1, 2) . . . .

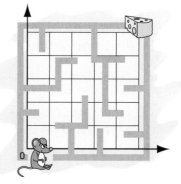

 2 ▶ **Scale Drawings**

This is a drawing of a train where **1 cm** represents **10 m**.

The actual length of the train is 9·5 × 10 = 95 m.

─ⓐ──────────────────────────────

1. These sunflowers are drawn to scale where 1 cm represents 100 cm.
   For each picture:
      i   measure the length shown
      ii calculate how tall each sunflower is.

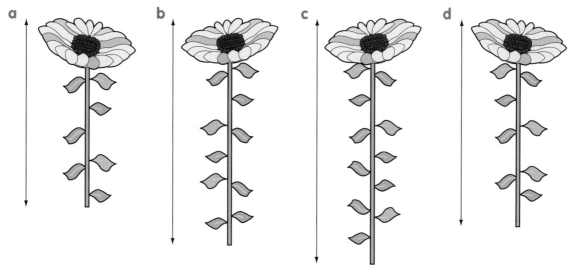

a   b   c   d

2. The actual bus represented by this scale drawing is 16 metres long.

   a Measure the length of the drawing.
   b What is the scale of the drawing?
   c What is the height of:
      i   the drawing
      ii the actual bus?

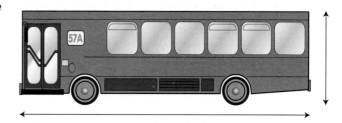

3. In a Primary 7's game of rounders, hoops were placed at positions
   A, B, C and D. Players run clockwise round from point to point.

   a Measure   i each marked angle   ii each marked length.
   b For each section of the run, calculate:
      i the bearing   ii the distance.

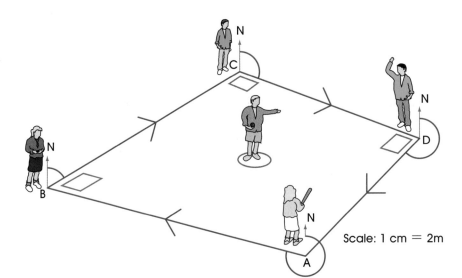

Scale: 1 cm = 2m

4. Two passenger ferries left Belfast Harbour at the same time.
   The Troon ferry left on a bearing of 060° and the Stranraer ferry on a
   bearing of 110°. Both ferries have sailed 30 km of the journey.
   Opposite is a sketch of the situation.

   a Make an accurate scale drawing
      using 1 cm to represent 5 km.
   b Measure the distance between
      the points P and Q.
   c What is the distance between the
      ships?
   d The accurate answer is 25·36 km.
      How close did you get?

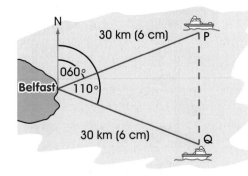

5. The Weymss Bay Ferry left the Isle of Cumbrae on a bearing of 070°
   and had travelled 6 km of its journey.
   A ferry going to Largs was on a 150° bearing from Cumbrae
   and had travelled 10 km so far.

   a Use the above information to make an accurate scale drawing
      of each ferry's route. Use the scale 1 cm = 1 km.
   b From your scale drawing, calculate the real distance between
      the ferries at this point of their journeys.

6. At NessieLand Theme Park, the cafe is 80 m away from the rollercoaster on a bearing of 300°.
   The water slide is 100 m away from the rollercoaster on a bearing of 220°.

   a Make an accurate scale drawing showing the position of the rollercoaster, cafe and water slide. Use the scale 1 cm = 10 m.
   b Use your drawing to calculate the real distance you would have to walk from the cafe to get to the water slide.

Challenge

Miss Grant went for a walk in the countryside with her dog.
She parked her car and walked 850 m to the lake on a bearing of 200°.
From the lake she walked 1 km to the picnic site for lunch on a bearing of 275° before returning to her car.

   a Using a scale of 1 cm = 100 m,
   make an accurate scale drawing of her walk.
   b Use your drawing to find:
      i the bearing of her car from the picnic site
      ii the distance from the picnic site back to her car.

B

1. Louise sees a steeple at a bearing of 045°.
   Jamie is 200 m east of Louise and can see the steeple on a bearing of 315°.
   Mark is standing halfway between Louise and Jamie.

   a Use this sketch to help you make an accurate scale drawing using a scale where 1 cm represents 20 m.

   b Calculate the distance of the steeple from Mark.

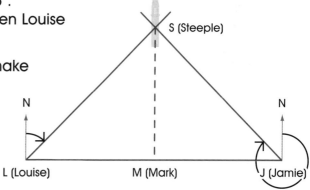

2. At a kite flying festival, Greg can see a large dragon kite by looking up through 25°. Nicola is 120 m east of Greg and can also see the same kite by looking up through 335°. Harry is standing exactly halfway between Greg and Nicola and right under the kite.

   a Make a rough sketch of the situation.
      Hint You should have an isosceles triangle.
   b Use this to help you make an accurate scale drawing, using a suitable scale.
   c How high is the dragon kite above Harry?

3. The *Ulysses* submarine detects a large object on the radar screen on a bearing of 325°. 40 miles west of *Ulysses*, another submarine, the *Poseidon* detects the same object on a bearing of 035°.

   a Using a scale 1 cm = 5 miles, make an accurate scale drawing of the situation.
   b How far is the object from: i the *Ulysses*   ii the *Poseidon*?

4. Jack walks his dog to the park from his home on a bearing of 150° for 600 m. He walks 800 m through the park to the shop on a bearing of 240° before returning home again.

   a Use this information to make an accurate scale drawing of Jack's walk.
   b Use your drawing to find:
      i   the bearing of his home from the shop
      ii the distance from the shop to his home.

5. A cargo boat sails from Hansel Harbour delivering goods to the Isles of Shanter and Moss. Shanter is 30 km away from the harbour on a bearing of 190°.

   From this Isle, the boat sails 25 km to Moss on a bearing of 280°.
   It then returns to Hansel Harbour.

   a Make an accurate scale drawing of the cargo boat's route.
     Pick your own scale.
   b From your drawing, calculate:
      i   the bearing of Hansel Harbour from the Isle of Moss
      ii the distance from Moss to the harbour.

Challenge

On a treasure hunt, a group are going from point to point picking up clues about where to go to next.

They identify the position of their next clue on their map.
It is 1·1 km away on a bearing of 160°.

After walking 400 m, they have to change direction to avoid marshland.
They continue walking 600 m on a bearing of 105°.

   a Make a scale drawing of the treasure hunt so far, using a suitable scale.
   b How far are they away from the next clue?
   c What is the bearing that will take the group to the clue?

3 ▶ Coordinates in Four Quadrants

The *x* and *y* axes divide
the coordinate plane into four parts.
The four parts are called quadrants.

A (3, 4) lies in the first quadrant.

B (−2, 3) lies in the second quadrant.

C (−4, −4) lies in the third quadrant.

D (1, −1) lies in the fourth quadrant.

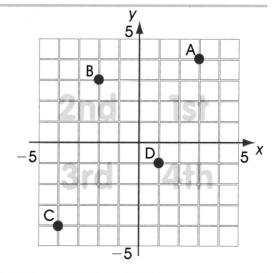

 A

1. In which quadrant do these points lie?

   a (−4, 5)   b (3, −1)   c (5, 2)   d (−5, −3)

2. Between which two quadrants do these points lie?

   a (−2, 0)   b (0, 5)   c (0, −3)   d (5, 0)

3. a Plot the following points on a coordinate diagram:

   P (−3, 3)   Q (−3, −3)   R (−4, −5)   S (2, −5)

   b Draw a line from P to Q.
   What are the coordinates of the point midway between P and Q?

   c What is the midpoint of RS?

4. Fido has buried his bone in the centre
   of a flower bed in the garden.
   This bed is hexagonal.
   The coordinates of its vertices taken
   in order are:

   (−2, 1)   (0, 1)   (1, −1)   (0, −3)
   (−2, −3)   (−3, −1)

   a Make a coordinate grid like the
   one shown.
   b Plot the points and draw the flower
   bed by joining each point to the
   next as you plot them.
   c Give the coordinates of Fido's bone.

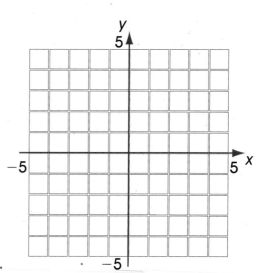

5. This arrow is pointing along the y-axis.

    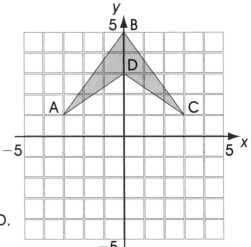

    a Write the coordinates of
    A, B, C and D.
    b The arrow rotates through 90°
    anticlockwise so that it ends up
    on the x-axis.
    Point B becomes (−5, 0).
    Write the coordinates of the new
    positions of A, C and D.
    c The arrow rotates again
    another 90° anticlockwise.
    List the new positions of A, B, C and D.

6. **a** On a coordinate grid, plot the points P (−4, 2), Q (−4, 4), R (−2, 4) and
        S (0, 0), and join them up in that order.
    b What shape have you drawn?

    c **i** Give the shape a quarter turn clockwise, keeping point S at (0, 0).
        ii Write down the coordinates of the new positions of P, Q and R.

    d Repeat **c** with the new shape.
    e Repeat again to complete the pattern.

7. A (−4, 3), B (−3, 1), C (0, 1), D (2, 0), E (0, −1), F (−3, −1) and G (−5, 1)
    are the vertices of a drawing of an aeroplane.

    a Plot the points to help you draw the aeroplane.
    b Add 3 to each *x*-coordinate and subtract 1 from each *y*-coordinate.

    For example, A (−1, 3) becomes (−1, 2).

    c Plot the new points to draw the aeroplane in a new position.

8. **a** On a coordinate diagram, plot the following points:

    A (−5, 0)   B (−4, 5)   C (0, 5)   D (−1, 0)

    b What shape is ABCD?

    c D moves to a new position D'. It moves three units to the left
        and two units down.
        What are the coordinates of D'?

    d **i** Draw lines from A to C and from B to D'.
        ii Give the coordinates of the point at which the lines intersect.

4 Calculating Distances along Grid Lines

A

1. We can use a coordinate diagram to help us calculate distances.

    Two horses graze in a field surrounded by a wooden fence.
    The scale of the drawing is that one unit represents 10 metres.

    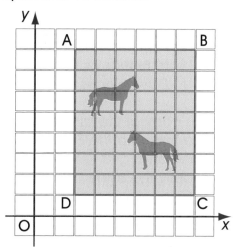

    a One section of fence runs from
       A (2, 8) to B (8, 8).
       i   How many units is this?
       ii How many metres does this
           represent?

    b Another section runs from D (2, 1) to A.
       i   How many units is this?
       ii How many metres does this
           represent?

    c What is the perimeter of the
       enclosure?

2. Two yachts sail to different islands.
    On the grid one unit represents 2 km.

    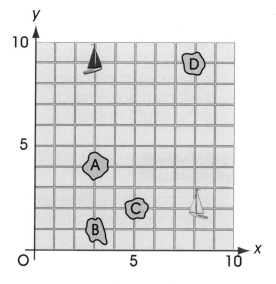

    a How far away is the:
       i   red yacht from Allow Isle (A)
       ii   red yacht from Breech Isle (B)
       iii yellow yacht from Cranna
            Isle (C)?

    b How much further does the
       yellow yacht have to travel to
       Doone Isle (D) than the red
       yacht does?

3. a On a coordinate diagram, draw the shape of Peter's garden by
       plotting the following points and joining them as you go:

       P (2, 3)   Q (2, 12)   R (10, 12)   S (10, 3)

    b Calculate the perimeter of Peter's garden if one unit represents 2 metres
       on the grid.

4. Here is a plan showing the positions of four friends' houses. To get from one house to another you can only go along grid lines. These represent the roads. One unit of the grid represents 10 m. Calculate the distance by road:

   a from Adam's house (A)
   to Bethany's house (B).
   b from Bethany's house
   to Carly's house (C).
   c from Adam's house to Carly's house.
   d from Bethany's house
   to David's house (D).

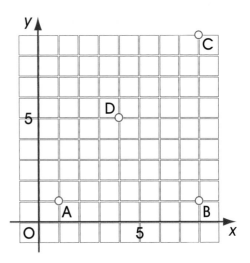

5. This copy of the famous painting *The Tree and the Fence* has been done on a grid to make sure it is exactly the same as the original painting. But the copy is smaller than the original.

   The scale of the grid is one unit represents 25 cm.
   Calculate:

   a the height of the tree
   in the original painting
   b the length of the fence
   in the original painting.

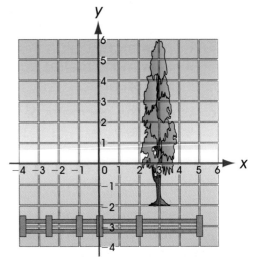

Challenge

a On a coordinate diagram, draw the outline of Southside Primary by joining the following points:

   A (−4, 4)   B (4, 4)   C (4, 1)
   D (−1, 1)   E (−1, −3)   F (−4, −3)

b Calculate the perimeter of the school if one unit represents 10 metres.

Unit 7 Fractions

I'll give you 2% of the money!

...or maybe even 0·03 (three hundredths) of the money?

...or would you prefer $\frac{1}{40}$ of the money?

Which of these do you think is the biggest share?

1 ▶ Looking Back

1. Draw a pentagon and shade in: **a** $\frac{1}{5}$ **b** $\frac{2}{5}$ **c** $\frac{6}{10}$

2. Simplify each fraction by dividing the top and bottom by the number in brackets:

   a $\frac{5}{15}(\div 5)$ **b** $\frac{21}{28}(\div 7)$ **c** $\frac{18}{48}(\div 6)$

3. Make each fraction as simple as you can:

   a $\frac{75}{100}$ **b** $\frac{42}{54}$ **c** $\frac{90}{100}$

4. Find the missing figure in each pair of equivalent fractions:

   a $\frac{3}{4} = \frac{?}{20}$ **b** $\frac{7}{8} = \frac{?}{24}$ **c** $\frac{7}{10} = \frac{?}{100}$ **d** $\frac{7}{20} = \frac{?}{100}$

5. **a** Find a fraction equivalent to $\frac{3}{4}$ with a denominator of 24.
   b Find a fraction equivalent to $\frac{5}{9}$ with a denominator of 81.
   c Find a fraction equivalent to $\frac{5}{6}$ with a denominator of 42.

6. $\frac{5}{6}$ of the 30 pupils in the class passed the test.

   a What is $\frac{1}{6}$ of 30?   **Hint** Divide by 6.
   b What is $\frac{5}{6}$ of 30?   **Hint** Multiply $\frac{1}{6}$ by 5.

7. $\frac{3}{8}$ of the 48 biscuits in the box were broken.

   a What is $\frac{1}{8}$ of 48?   **Hint** Divide by 8.
   b What is $\frac{3}{8}$ of 48?   **Hint** Multiply $\frac{1}{8}$ by 3.

8. Calculate each amount:

   a $\frac{2}{5}$ of 45   b $\frac{3}{4}$ of 12   c $\frac{2}{7}$ of 14

9. $\frac{2}{5} = 2 \div 5 = 0.4$

   In a similar way write each common fraction as an equivalent decimal fraction:

   a $\frac{3}{5}$ b $\frac{7}{10}$ c $\frac{1}{4}$ d $\frac{3}{4}$

10. Write each of these as an equivalent decimal fraction:

    a $\frac{25}{100}$ b $\frac{65}{100}$ c $\frac{9}{100}$ d $\frac{1}{100}$

11. Write each of these as an equivalent percentage:

    a $\frac{40}{100}$ b $\frac{25}{100}$ c $\frac{5}{100}$ d $\frac{1}{100}$

12. Write the following percentages in decimal form:

    a 20%   b 10%   c 90%   d 9%

2 Fractions of Measurements

Example Find $\frac{2}{5}$ of a kilogram.   **Example** Find $\frac{3}{4}$ of an hour.

$\frac{2}{5}$ of a kilogram $= \frac{2}{5}$ of 1000 g $\frac{3}{4}$ of an hour $= \frac{3}{4}$ of 60 min
$= 1000 \div 5 \times 2$ $= 60 \div 4 \times 3$
$= 200 \times 2$ $= 15 \times 3$
$= 400$ g $= 45$ minutes

A

1. Calculate the following, giving your answers in grams:

   a $\frac{1}{4}$ kg   b $\frac{1}{5}$ kg   c $\frac{1}{10}$ kg   d $\frac{1}{20}$ kg   e $\frac{1}{50}$ kg
   f $\frac{1}{100}$ kg   g $\frac{1}{200}$ kg   h $\frac{1}{500}$ kg   i $\frac{3}{4}$ kg   j $\frac{4}{5}$ kg
   k $\frac{7}{10}$ kg   l $\frac{3}{20}$ kg   m $\frac{9}{50}$ kg   n $\frac{3}{100}$ kg   o $\frac{3}{200}$ kg

2. James opens a 2 kg bag of sugar.
   He pours $\frac{1}{4}$ of the bag into a bowl.

   a How many grams is this?
   b He pours $\frac{2}{5}$ of the bag into a storage jar.
      How many grams are poured into the jar?
   c He spills $\frac{1}{10}$ of the bag. How many grams has he lost?
   d How many grams are left in the bag?

3. Calculate the following, giving your answers in millilitres:

   a $\frac{3}{5}$ litre   b $\frac{1}{8}$ litre   c $\frac{3}{10}$ litre   d $\frac{7}{20}$ litre   e $\frac{21}{50}$ litre   f $\frac{77}{100}$ litre

4. An urn is used to make up the orange juice at the school fête. The urn holds 20 litres.

   a $\frac{1}{4}$ of the urn is used by the helpers. How many millilitres is this?

   b $\frac{2}{5}$ was used by children at the cake stall. How many millilitres is this?

   c The head teacher thinks that $\frac{3}{8}$ of the urn will be needed for parents.
      i How many millilitres are needed?
      ii What is the total amount of juice needed? Comment.

5. Calculate the following, giving your answers in minutes:

   a $\frac{1}{6}$ hour   b $\frac{1}{12}$ hour   c $\frac{7}{10}$ hour   d $\frac{9}{30}$ hour   e $\frac{5}{12}$ hour   f $\frac{2}{15}$ hour

6. Isabel has a 3 hour video tape. $\frac{1}{6}$ is used to record a comedy. $\frac{1}{3}$ is used for a play. $\frac{2}{5}$ is used for a documentary.
   Is there enough of the tape left to record a 15 minute cartoon?

 B

1. $\frac{3}{7}$ of a cake is eaten.

   a What fraction is left?
   b The cake originally weighed 490 g. What weight is left?

2. Duncan had walked $\frac{3}{8}$ of the way to school.

   a What fraction of the distance does he still have to walk?
   b The distance between his home and school is 2·4 km. How far has he still to walk: i in kilometres   ii in metres?

3. A runner pulled a muscle after $\frac{11}{20}$ of a race.

   a What fraction of the race was yet to be run?
   b It was the 5000 m. How many metres from the finish line did his accident happen?

4. In a marathon Peter kept up with the leaders for $\frac{2}{15}$ of the time.

 a For what fraction of the time was he behind the leaders.
 b Peter's total time for the race was 3 hours and 30 minutes.
  i Write this in minutes.
  ii For how many minutes did he keep up with the leaders?

5. In Information Handling, when working with fractions, the most useful diagram is the pie chart.

 Fern asked her class about their preference in chocolate.
 $\frac{5}{9}$ liked dark chocolate, $\frac{1}{3}$ preferred milk chocolate and $\frac{1}{9}$ didn't like chocolate at all. Fern drew a pie chart to represent the whole class.
 There are 360° round the centre of the circle.

 a Calculate: i $\frac{5}{9}$ of 360   ii $\frac{1}{3}$ of 360
          iii $\frac{1}{9}$ of 360.

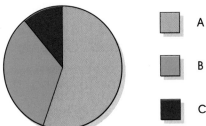

A

B

C

 b What angle will represent those who:
  i preferred dark chocolate
  ii preferred milk chocolate?

 c Here the chart has been drawn.
  Which sector goes with which set of people?

6. Mr Ferguson asked his class what they preferred to watch on TV.
 $\frac{3}{10}$ liked cartoons, $\frac{3}{5}$ sport and $\frac{1}{10}$ films.

 a In a pie chart, what angle would be needed to represent:
  i those who liked cartoons   ii those who preferred sport?

 b Can you work out the angle that represents those who preferred films without using fractions?

Challenge

Children were asked the colour of their mobile phone.
$\frac{1}{4}$ said red, $\frac{1}{3}$ said blue and $\frac{3}{8}$ said purple.

 a In a pie chart, what angle would be needed to represent:
  i red phones   ii blue phones   iii purple phones?

 b What is the total number of degrees used so far?

 c i How many degrees are unaccounted for?
  ii $\frac{\text{this number}}{360}$ is the fraction who don't have a phone.
   Write this fraction in its simplest form.

3 ▸ Common Fraction, Decimal Fraction, Percentage

◂ A ▸

1. Express the following as percentages and then as decimal fractions:

   a $\frac{1}{2}$ b $\frac{1}{4}$ c $\frac{1}{5}$ d $\frac{1}{10}$ e $\frac{1}{100}$ f $\frac{2}{2}$ g $\frac{3}{4}$ h $\frac{4}{5}$ i $\frac{9}{10}$

2. Express the following as percentages correct to one decimal place:

   a $\frac{3}{7}$ b $\frac{2}{9}$ c $\frac{1}{3}$ d $\frac{2}{3}$ e $\frac{7}{8}$

3. Express each percentage as a fraction of 100 and then simplify:

   a 25%   b 50%   c 20%   d 75%
   e 10%   f 40%   g 15%   h 80%

4. Calculate:

   a 10% of £390   b 75% of £672   c 40% of £825
   d 60% of £7000   e 4% of £90

5. During a survey of 400 people over the age of 30,
   it was discovered that 12% had suffered mumps.

   a How many people is this?
   b 16% of them had had measles but not mumps. How many people is this?
   c Although they had not suffered from measles or mumps, 17% said they
     had had German measles. Calculate how many people this is.
   d What percentage of those asked had never had any of the three diseases?
     How many is this?

6. In a survey about favourite crisp flavours, 1600 people were asked to pick
   just one flavour.
   The table shows the findings:

Crisp Flavour	Percentage who prefer it
Tomato	13%
Smokey Bacon	18%
Cheese and Onion	14%
Plain	

   a How many preferred: i tomato   ii cheese and onion?
   b Anyone who didn't choose tomato, smokey bacon or cheese and
     onion answered "plain".
     i What percentage was this?
     ii How many people was this?

Some percentage calculations are easy to do if you remember these simple facts:

$$\frac{1}{2} = 50\% \qquad \frac{1}{3} = 33\frac{1}{3}\% \qquad \frac{1}{4} = 25\%$$

$$\frac{1}{5} = 20\% \qquad \frac{1}{10} = 10\% \qquad \frac{1}{100} = 1\%$$

B

1. Calculate, without any written working:

   a 50% of £200   b 33$\frac{1}{3}$% of £21   c 25% of £80   d 20% of £300
   e 10% of £780   f 1% of £500   g 20% of £10   h 10% of £79
   i 25% of £28   j 50% of £46   k 25% of £72   l 33$\frac{1}{3}$% of £201
   m 1% of £350   n 100% of £70   o 20% of £45

2. Jill saw a toaster with a '15% off' sticker. The marked price was £40.

   a i Work out 10% of £40
     ii Halve this to work out 5% of £40.
     iii Add these two answers to find 15% of £40.

   b There were other goods being sold with the same offer.

   Use the method above to find 15% of each amount.

   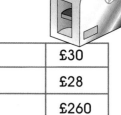

i	Kettle	£60	ii	Breadmaker	£30
iii	CD player	£90	iv	Iron	£28
v	Portable TV	£150	vi	Fridge	£260
vii	Washing Machine	£450	viii	Battery pack	£4·80
ix	Light bulbs (12)	£3·60	x	CD-ROM	£7·20

Challenge

The government charges 17$\frac{1}{2}$% tax on goods.
The original price of the toaster above was £40.

   a i What is 10% of 40?
     ii Halve this to get 5% of 40.
     iii Halve this to get 2$\frac{1}{2}$% of 40
     iv Add all three answers to get 17$\frac{1}{2}$% of 40.

   b Work out the tax on all the original prices of the electrical goods in question **2**.

Unit 8 — Whole Numbers

What 2-digit number can be divided by the greatest number of whole numbers … with no remainder?

No, it's 80!

96

36

I say 48

1 Looking Back

1. More people live in California than in any other U.S. state.
   Its population is 33 609 700.
   Its land area is 411 033 km².
   Write both numbers in words.

2. The state of Texas has the second highest population.
   Twenty million, three hundred and eighty-five thousand, four hundred and fifty people live there.
   Its land area is *six hundred and ninety-one thousand, and three* km².
   Write both numbers in figures.

3. The table shows the populations of some other American states:

State	Alabama	Arizona	Colorado	Kentucky	Minnesota	S. Carolina
Population	4 387 650	4 893 170	4 145 800	3 989 800	4 823 200	3 932 900

Write the populations in order, largest first.

8. There are 36 biscuits in every packet of *Bisco's*.

   a How many packets of *Bisco's* can be obtained from 1000 biscuits?

   b How many biscuits are left over?

9. a 38 beads are needed to make a Princess necklace.

   i How many Princess necklaces can be made with 500 beads?

   ii How many beads are left over?

   b A Duchess necklace needs only 32 beads.

   i How many Duchess necklaces can be made with 500 beads?

   ii How many beads are left over?

Challenge

There are 831 056 wage earners on the island of Caledonia.
The people on the island wish to build a new Parliament building.
The cost of the building is estimated at £47 650 000.
All wage earners are asked to pay an equal share of the cost of the new building.

The calculation is done and the amount each wage earner is asked to pay is rounded to the nearest £1.

   a By how much is the money raised short of the required amount?

   b If every wage earner is asked to pay £1 more, how much more than the cost of the building will be raised?

 Factors

A whole number that divides another, **without a remainder**, is said to be a **factor** of the second whole number.

| Example | 1, 2, 5 and 10 divide 10, without a remainder, so 1, 2, 5 and 10 are the factors of 10. |

Factors of 10									
1	2	3	4	5	6	7	8	9	10
✓	✓	✗	✗	✓	✗	✗	✗	✗	✓

 A

1. List all the factors of:

   a 6   b 8   c 12   d 14   e 15   f 18   g 24   h 25
   i 28   j 30   k 38   l 42   m 50   n 68   o 83   p 100

2. **a** 120 has sixteen factors. 1, 2, 3, 4, 5, 6, 8 and 10 are eight of them.
Find the other eight factors of 120.

  Hint Find how many times 10, 8, 6, 5, 4, 3, 2 and 1 divide 120.

  b 144 has fifteen factors. 1, 2, 3, 4, 6, 8, 9 and 12 are eight of them.
Find the other seven factors of 144.

  c 1, 2, 7 and 11 are four factors of 154. Find the other four factors of 154.

3. Find all the factors of: **a** 172   **b** 270   **c** 400.

4. What factors do 52 and 65 have in common?

5. What are the common factors of 84 and 102?

6. 12 can be written as $2 \times 2 \times 3$.
The number 12 has been **factorised**.
In the same way, factorise: **a** 40   **b** 82   **c** 150.

5 ▶ Prime Numbers

If a number has only two factors – the number itself and 1 – then it is said to be
a **prime number**.

  7 is a prime number because **1** and **7** are the only factors of **7**.
  15 is not a prime number because it can also be divided by **3**.
  1 is not a prime number because it only has **1** factor.

1. Write down the numbers less than 20 that have exactly two factors.
You should find eight of them.
These are the **prime numbers** less than 20.

2. Which of these numbers are prime numbers?
Give a reason for your answer.

  a 30   **b** 35   **c** 37   **d** 39   **e** 43   **f** 87   **g** 101

3. Write down all the even numbers that are prime.

4. The first two whole numbers ending in 7 are prime numbers.
They are 7 and 17.
Which of the next eight whole numbers ending in 7 are prime numbers?

5.

The Sieve of Eratosthenes

A Greek Mathematician called Eratosthenes, who lived over 2000 years ago, invented a way to find prime numbers.
He used a 100 square.

a Make a 100 square as shown or use Resource Sheet 8·1.

b Score out 1.
(It is not prime as it doesn't have two factors.)

c Circle the first number not scored out (2) and then score out every number that can be divided by 2.

d Circle the first number not scored out (3) and then score out every number that can be divided by 3.

e Circle the first number not scored out (5) and then score out every number that can be divided by 5.

f Keep going until you run out of numbers.

You will have circled all the prime numbers between 1 and 100.

Situation after step **e**.

6. Which of these numbers are prime numbers?
Give a reason for your answer.

    a 153   **b** 161   **c** 167   **d** 173   **e** 187

7. Which factors of the following numbers are prime numbers?

    a 32   **b** 40   **c** 92   **d** 140   **e** 144

8. Find a whole number that doesn't have any factors that are prime numbers.

Algebra

Unit 9

Diophantus of Alexandria was born in Greece around 200 AD and died around 280 AD.

Diophantus is known as The father of Algebra.
He developed his own shorthand way of writing the solutions to maths problems. This shorthand led to people using letters to represent numbers.
We call this algebra.

DIOPHANTI
ALEXANDRINI
ARITHMETICORVM
LIBRI SEX
ET DE NVMERIS MVLTANGVLIS
LIBER VNVS
CVMCOMMENTARIS CG BACHETI VC

TOLOSE

One of Diophantus' books was called Arithmetica

This picture shows the front page of the 1670 edition of Arithmetica

1 Looking Back

1. If $x = 5$, give the value of:

   a $x - 2$ b $x + 3$ c $15 - x$ d $x + x$
   e $4x$ f $\frac{1}{5}x$ g $3x - 2$ h $7x + 6$

2. Write down the expressions marked by a question mark in each machine:

   a   IN y → **Subtract 4** → ?   OUT

   b   IN m → **Add 9** → ?   OUT

   c   IN n → **Multiply by 8** → ?   OUT

   d   IN z → **Halve** → ?   OUT

3. Write expressions for the total for each set of cards:

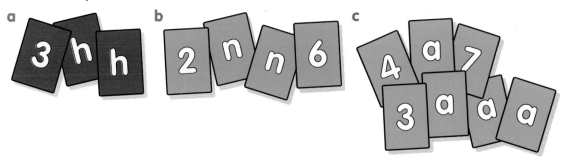

a 3 h h

b 2 n n 6

c 4 a 7 3 a a a

4. A plank was 5 m long.
   A piece *x* m long was sawn off.
   What length is left?

5. There are *y* litres of liquid in a bottle.
   2 more litres are added.
   How many litres are now in the bottle?

6. There are *m* flags.
   How many stars are there?

7. There are *k* hands. How many fingers
   (including thumbs) are there?

8. There are *x* bicycles.
   How many wheels are there?

2 Replacing Letters with Numbers

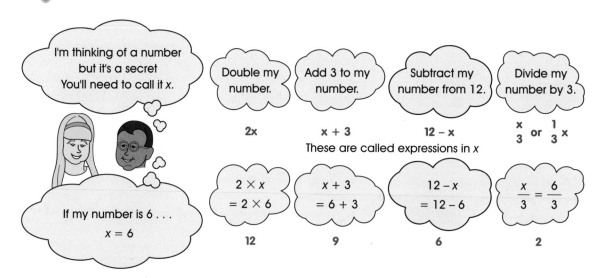

In each **expression**, 6 has been **substituted** for *x*. The expression has then
been **evaluated**.

We can use number machines to show these steps:

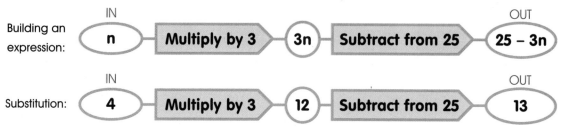

A

1. The first number machine builds an expression.
   The second number machine evaluates the expression.
   Copy and complete:

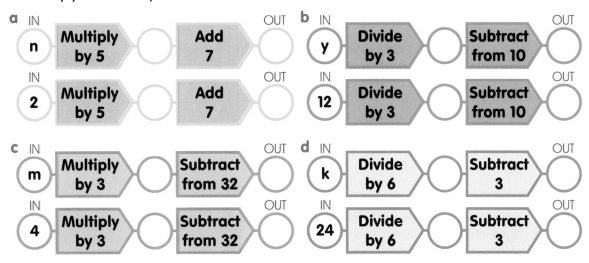

2. Evaluate each expression for the value given:

   a $2y - 3$ when $y = 4$ b $13 - 2y$ when $y = 1$ c $1 + \frac{1}{2}k$ when $k = 8$
   d $8 - \frac{1}{4}y$ when $y = 12$ e $15 + 6t$ when $t = 3$ f $\frac{1}{6}n + 3$ when $n = 48$
   g $5r - 7$ when $r = 3$ h $12 + 8y$ when $y = 8$ i $12 - \frac{x}{3}$ when $x = 15$

3. Find the expressions described:

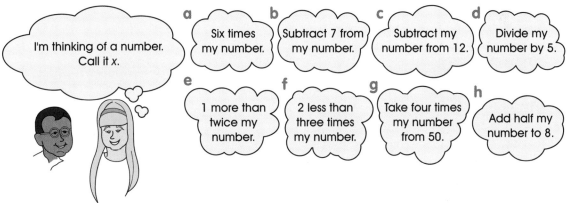

   I'm thinking of a number. Call it x.

   a Six times my number.
   b Subtract 7 from my number.
   c Subtract my number from 12.
   d Divide my number by 5.
   e 1 more than twice my number.
   f 2 less than three times my number.
   g Take four times my number from 50.
   h Add half my number to 8.

4. If $x = 10$, evaluate each expression in question 3.

5. a Find an expression for the total cost in £ for these six items.
   b If $m = 8$ and $n = 2$, what is the total cost?
   c If $m = 11$ and $n = 5$, what is the total cost?

Vase £m Vase £m Pot £n Pot £n Vase £m Vase £m

6. **a** Find an expression for the total area covered by these tiles.

b If $a = 0.5$ and $b = 1$, what is the total area?

c If $a = 0.7$ and $b = 0.9$, what is the total area?

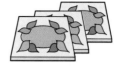

Area of 1 tile: a m²

Area of 1 tile: b m²

7. This wooden crate has vertical slats of length v metres and horizontal slats of length h metres.

a Find an expression for the total length of all the slats that make up the crate.

b If $v = 2$ and $h = 1$, find the total length of the slats.

c If $v = 1.8$ and $h = 1.5$, what is the total length?

8. **a** Find an expression for the total volume of all five barrels.

b If $k = 500$ and $w = 250$, find the total volume of the barrels.

c If $k = 750$ and $h = 550$, find the total volume.

Volume of each barrel is k litres

Volume of each barrel is w litres

9. Find the value of each expression if $x = 2$, $y = 6$, $z = 5$ and $w = 10$.

a $3x - 6$ **b** $13 - 2y$ **c** $xz - w$ **d** $3z - w$ **e** $wx - 4x$

f $2z + 7w$ **g** $\frac{1}{2}(w + y)$ **h** $\frac{w + x}{4}$ **i** $xy + \frac{w}{2}$ **j** $4(w - 2x)$

k $\frac{1}{3}(2z - 1)$ **l** $\frac{3w - y}{3}$ **m** $2x + 3y - z$ **n** $\frac{1}{2}w - x - \frac{1}{2}y$

o $\frac{4x + w}{y}$ **p** $2(yz - xw)$ **q** $3yw$ **r** $\frac{5xy - 4z}{w}$ **s** $\frac{w + x}{z - x}$

Challenge

The Star Challenge

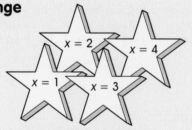

$x = 2$ $x = 4$ $x = 1$ $x = 3$

$y = 3$ $y = 5$ $y = 4$ $y = 6$

Which is the correct value for x . . .

. . . and which is the correct value for y?

The clue is that all of these expressions give positive whole numbers:

 $3y - 4x$

 $\frac{xy + y}{2}$

 $\frac{1}{3}(2x + y)$

 $\frac{y + x}{y - x}$

There is only one pair of substitutions that will work.

Simplifying Expressions

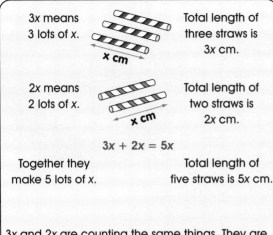

3x means 3 lots of x.		Total length of three straws is 3x cm.
2x means 2 lots of x.		Total length of two straws is 2x cm.

$3x + 2x = 5x$

Together they make 5 lots of x.

Total length of five straws is 5x cm.

3x and 2x are counting the same things. They are **like terms** and so 3x + 2x can be simplified by adding to get 5x.

3x means 3 lots of x.		Total length of three straws is 3x cm.
4y means 4 lots of y.		Total length of four straws is 4y cm.

$3x + 4y$

Together they make 3 lots of x and 4 lots of y

Total length of seven straws is (3x + 4y) cm.

3x and 4y are counting different things. They are **unlike terms** and so 3x + 4y cannot be simplified by adding.

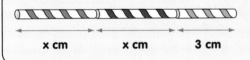

Total length of three straws is (x + x + 3) cm.
Since x and x are **like** terms this simplifies to (2x + 3) cm.
2x and 3 are **unlike** terms so 2x + 3 cannot be simplified.

x cm   **x cm**   **3 cm**

 A

1. **a** For each rectangle, write a simplified expression for its perimeter (that is, the total length of the straws).

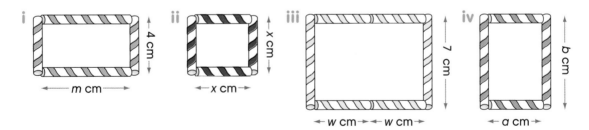

b Evaluate the expression for each perimeter using these substitutions:

i $m = 5$ ii $x = 8$
iii $w = 3$ iv $a = 4$ and $b = 5$

2. Match each arrow with a destination on the target by simplifying the expressions:

a

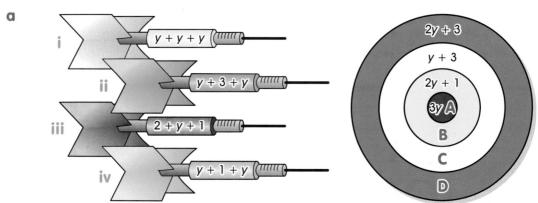

b Evaluate each target expression A, B, C and D for:
  i $y = 2$ **ii** $y = 5$ **iii** $y = 9$

3. **a** Place each counter on the correct square:

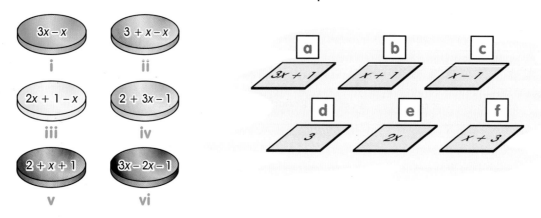

b Find the value of each square when: **i** $x = 1$ **ii** $x = 2$ **iii** $x = 3$.
c Find the smallest whole number replacement for x that gives each square a different value from all the other squares.

4. Simplify each expression by collecting like terms:

  a $m + 1 + m + 1$ **b** $x + 1 + x + 5 + x$ **c** $2y + z + y - z$
  d $4a + 2b - b + a$ **e** $5w + 6 - 3w - 2$ **f** $4x + y + 3x - y$
  g $c + 2 + 5c - 1 + c$ **h** $7k + m - 4k + 3m + 2$

5. Find the value of each expression in question **4** for the following substitutions:

  a $m = 3$ **b** $x = 2$ **c** $y = 1$ and $z = 4$ **d** $a = 5$ and $b = 2$
  e $w = 7$ **f** $x = 10$ and $y = 5$ **g** $c = 8$ **h** $k = 3$ and $m = 9$

B

1. Simplify each expression and find its value using the given substitution:

   a $5x + 4y - 3x - 2y$ $x = 6$ and $y = 3$
   b $5a + 3b - 3a - b$ $a = 7$ and $b = 5$
   c $3m + 8n - 2m - 3n$ $m = 15$ and $n = 14$
   d $5 + 2r + 5t - r - 4t$ $r = 2$ and $t = 9$
   e $6y + 2w - 4y - w + y$ $w = 16$ and $y = 11$
   f $\frac{1}{2}x + 4y + \frac{1}{2}x - 3y$ $x = 13$ and $y = 27$

2. a Find a simplified expression for the perimeter of the frame of this picture. The measurements are in centimetres.
   b If $x = 17$, calculate the perimeter.
   c The length and breadth of the inside frame of the picture each measure 2 cm less than the outside.
   Find an expression for the inside perimeter.
   d Find an expression for the total of the inside and outside perimeters.

   $x + 3$

   $x + 5$

3. For each frame:

   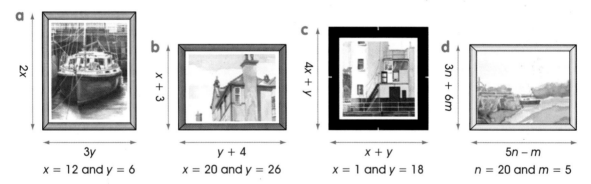

   a $2x$ $3y$ $x = 12$ and $y = 6$
   b $x + 3$ $y + 4$ $x = 20$ and $y = 26$
   c $4x + y$ $x + y$ $x = 1$ and $y = 18$
   d $3n + 6m$ $5n - m$ $n = 20$ and $m = 5$

   i find an expression for the perimeter
   ii calculate its value for the given substitution.
   The measurements are in centimetres.

4. A small enclosure consists of vertical slats and horizontal supports.
   Each vertical slat is 12 cm longer than each horizontal support.

   a If each horizontal support has length x cm, what is the length of a vertical slat?
   b Write an expression for the total length, in cm, of the slats and supports.
   c If $x = 120$, what is this total length in metres?

Challenge

The Cascade

Routes can only be downwards to the left or right.
As you pass through an expression, add it to your total.

1. There is only one route to get Total A.
   What is this total?

2. What is Total D?

3. How many different routes are there
   to get Total B?
   Find all the possibilities for Total B.

4. Find the possibilities for Total C.

5. When $x = 1$ and $y = 1$, there are
   just two routes that give the same
   total. Find them.

6. For $x = 3$ and $y = 5$, again there are just two routes with the same
   total. Can you find them?

7. Can you find a pair of values for x and y that makes three or more
   routes have the same total?

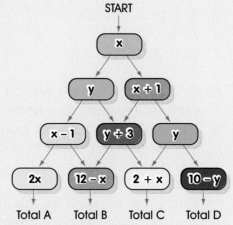

START

x

y $x + 1$

$x - 1$ $y + 3$ y

$2x$ $12 - x$ $2 + x$ $10 - y$

Total A Total B Total C Total D

4 Keeping Numbers in Order

Calculate:

$1 + 2 \times 3$

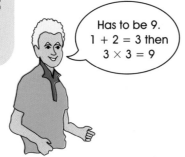

Has to be 9.
$1 + 2 = 3$ then
$3 \times 3 = 9$

When I was at school
$\times$ came before $+$.
So that gives $1 + 6 = 7$

There is an agreed order when doing a group of calculations:

So who is right?

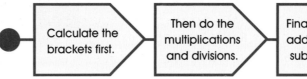

Calculate the
brackets first.

Then do the
multiplications
and divisions.

Finally do any
additions and
subtractions.

A

1. Do these calculations:

   a $(2 - 1) \times (4 - 3)$

   b $\dfrac{1 + 3}{4 - 2}$

   c $2 + 1 \times 4 - 3$

   d $\dfrac{4 \times 3}{2 + 1}$

   e $4 + \dfrac{3}{1 + 2}$

   f $\dfrac{4 \times 3}{2 \times 1}$

   g $4 + 3 \times (2 - 1)$

   h $\dfrac{4 \times (3 + 1)}{2}$

   i $(4 - 1) \times 2 + 3$

   j $4 \times 3 - 2 \times 1$

2. Each calculation in question **1** uses 1, 2, 3 and 4.
   The answers give all the whole numbers from 1 to 10.
   Construct calculations using 1, 2, 3 and 4 to give 11 to 16.

3. If $a = 1$, $b = 2$, $c = 3$ and $d = 4$, sort these expressions into order of increasing value:

   a $c + b \times (d - a)$

   b $\dfrac{c \times d}{a + b}$

   c $\dfrac{(a + c) \times d}{b}$

   d $d + (b - a) \times c$

   e $(b - a) \times (d - c)$

   f $\dfrac{c}{a + b} + d$

   g $\dfrac{a + c}{d - b}$

   h $d \times c - a \times b$

   i $\dfrac{c \times d}{b \times a}$

   j $b + a \times d - c$

◆ **Investigate**

The Digit Century

Using 1, 2, 3 and 4 can you create calculations that give the numbers 1 to 100?
Try to create a class record: how far can you get from 1 with no gaps?
Make a chart showing the solutions to each of the numbers.
Can you find different solutions for the same number?

The Rules

❖ The digits 1, 2, 3 and 4 all have to appear exactly once in each calculation.

❖ The operations $+$, $-$, $\times$ and $\div$ may be used.

❖ Brackets may be used.

❖ You are allowed to join the digits. For example, 1 and 2 can be joined to form 12.

❖ The $\sqrt{}$ sign may be used. For example, $\sqrt{4}$ uses the digit 4 to give 2.

❖ Powers are allowed. For example 3^2 makes 9 and uses the digits 2 and 3.

❖ Decimal points are allowed. For example, $\cdot 1$. **Hint** Try dividing by $\cdot 1$.

Information Handling

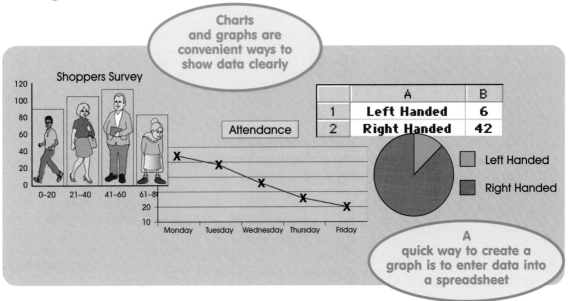

1 Looking Back

1. The number of fans attending Rovers football ground was recorded for six games.

Game	1	2	3	4	5	6
Attendance	11 321	12 150	13 020	14 102	14 340	15 434

a Draw a line graph to display this data.

b Describe the trend shown by the graph.

c How do you think Rovers performed over the season?

d At one of the matches, two thirds of the fans were Rovers supporters and one third were supporting the other team.

Draw a pie chart to display this data.

2. Joanne was training to compete in a triathlon event. This involves swimming, cycling and running. Her timed training diary for each event is shown.

Swimming

Week	Time (min:sec)
1	42:15
2	42:05
3	41:57
4	41:43
5	41:35
6	41:28
7	41:20
8	41:16
9	41:08
10	41:00

Cycling

Week	Time (min:sec)
1	1:51
2	1:48
3	1:57
4	1:55
5	1:52
6	1:53
7	1:54
8	1:51
9	1:50
10	1:51

Running

Week	Time (min:sec)
1	59:23
2	58:30
3	57:42
4	56:54
5	56:51
6	56:50
7	56:47
8	56:48
9	56:45
10	56:45

a i Copy and complete the line graph to display the swimming results.

ii What is the purpose of the zig-zag on the Time axis?

iii Explain why the y-axis does not show the numbers 41:60 or 41:70.

iv Describe the trend shown by the graph.

b i Draw a line graph to display the cycling times.

ii Describe the trend shown by the graph.

c i Draw a line graph to display the running times.

ii Describe the trend shown by the graph.

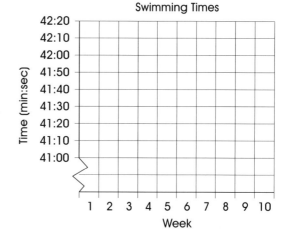

3. During the race, Joanne spent $\frac{1}{8}$ of the time swimming, $\frac{1}{4}$ of the time running and $\frac{5}{8}$ of the time cycling.
Draw a pie chart to display these results.

2 Line Graphs

A

1. The outside temperature was measured and recorded every hour.

Time	9:00	10:00	11:00	12:00	13:00	14:00	15:00
Temp. (°C)	8	10	13	15	15	14	13

  a Draw a line graph to display this data.
  b Is it possible to use the graph to tell the temperature at exactly 10:30?
      Explain your answer.
  c Describe the trend shown by the graph.

2. When Mr McLaren has his porridge in the morning, he likes it to be quite
hot, around 60°C.

He never seems to get it quite right and decides to investigate. The
temperature of the water is recorded every 30 seconds as it heats. As the
water heats, the change is expected to be gradual. The results are
recorded below:

Time (seconds)	0	30	60	90	120	150
Temp. (°C)	20	27	37	52	70	91

  a Draw a line graph to display the data, joining the points with a smooth
      curve.
  b For how many minutes would you advise Mr McLaren to set his cooker
      timer in order fully to enjoy his porridge?

3. Lindsay plants a seedling and measures its height every month, for a year.
The results are recorded below:

Month	May	June	July	Aug	Sept	Oct	Nov	Dec	Jan	Feb	March	April
Height (cm)	8·5	19	32·5	48·5	69	88	97	101·5	104	107	110·5	112

  a Draw a line graph to display this data, joining the points with a smooth
      curve.
  b Describe the growth pattern.
  c Do you think that the height of the plant is related to its age, in months?

4. The data below shows the flight distance and fuel used
   for various flights in the same type of aeroplane.
   The flights have been sorted by the fuel used, in ascending order.

   a Make a line graph to display the data.
   b Describe the relationship between distance flown and fuel used.

Journey	Distance (nautical miles)	Fuel (gallons)
Amsterdam–Cointrin	400	200
Bangkok–Hong Kong	973	500
Geneva–Athens	1053	600
Athens–Kuwait	1425	700
Bombay–Bangkok	1642	750
Montreal–Reykjavik	2056	900

5. One kilogram of *Pic'n'mix* sweets costs £3·60.

   a Copy and complete the table:

Number of kilograms	0·5	1	1·5	2	2·5	3	3·5	4
Cost (£)		3·60					12·60	

   b The two quantities, number of kilograms and cost, are in direct proportion.
      Draw a straight line graph of the data to show this relationship.

◆ **Investigate**

Investigate the relationship between the **length of sides** of a square and
the **perimeter** of a square.

   a Copy and complete the table:

Length of Side (cm)	1	2	3	4	5	6	7	8	9	10
Perimeter (cm)	4									

   b Draw a line graph of the data.
   c Describe the relationship shown between the quantities.

If you have access to a computer, try questions **1** to **5** and the
Investigation on a spreadsheet.

Choose the correct sort of graph required from the **chart** menu.

Print out your graphs and compare them to the graphs you have drawn
for each question.

4. Some pupils at Westerlees Primary School decided to investigate the birthday seasons of the pupils within their school. There are 200 pupils in the school.

They found that 60 pupils were born in spring, 50 pupils were born in summer, 30 pupils were born in autumn and the rest were born in winter.

a Here is how they calculated the percentages of pupils born in spring:

Spring $= \frac{60}{200} = \frac{60}{200} \times 100\% = 30\%$

Calculate the percentages for:
i summer   ii autumn   iii winter

b Draw a pie chart to display the results.

◆ Investigate

Carry out an investigation about the birthday seasons of pupils in your class or school.
Calculate the figures as percentages.
Draw a pie chart to display the results.
Write a short summary comparing your results with those of the pupils in question **4**.

If you have access to a computer, create a new spreadsheet file and enter the data from the birthday seasons results as pupil numbers.
Highlight the data and choose to create a pie chart from the chart menu.
Print your chart.

	A	B
1	Spring	60
2	Summer	50
3	Autumn	30
4	Winter	

Create a new spreadsheet file and enter the data from the birthday seasons results as percentage figures. Highlight the data and choose to create a pie chart from the chart menu.
Print your chart.

	A	B
1	Spring	30
2	Summer	25
3	Autumn	15
4	Winter	30
5		

Compare both pie charts. What do you notice? Can you explain?

Unit 11 Decimals

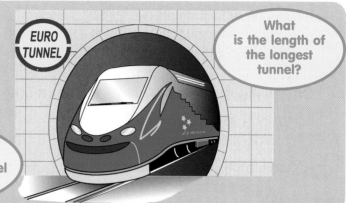

The Channel Tunnel opened in 1991 and runs from Folkestone, England to Calais, France.

It is 49·9 km in length, which is more than 65 times the length of the Clyde Tunnel (0·760 km).

EURO TUNNEL

What is the length of the longest tunnel?

Find out which country has the longest tunnel in the world.

 Looking Back

1. Round each of the following numbers to the nearest whole number:

   a 17·8   b 37·7   c 98·5   d 123·3   e 396·5   f 499·6
   g 7·81   h 55·09   i 9·55   j 30·79   k 99·51

2. Round each of the following to: i the nearest 10   ii the nearest 100:

   a 423·2 m   b 192·6 kg   c £87·25   d 125·5 cm
   e 480·9 g   f 427·4 kg   g 218·2 litres

3. Estimate the answer to the following by rounding each term in the calculation to the nearest whole number.

   Example   14·6 + 8·3 is about 15 + 8, so 14·6 + 8·3 is about 23.

   a 11·7 + 9·2   b 18·2 + 7·6   c 20·7 − 13·5   d 31·13 − 7·77
   e 27·7 + 15·11   f 41·6 + 15·5   g 35·29 − 12·3   h 41·4 − 12·55
   i 33·5 + 9·7   j 25·6 + 18·32   k 27·7 + 16·4   l 50·81 − 11·7

4. Calculate:

   a 16·3 × 10   b 34·67 × 10   c 18·3 ÷ 10   d 10·9 ÷ 10
   e 81·03 × 10   f 100·4 ÷ 10   g 1·45 × 100   h 11·08 × 100
   i 12 ÷ 100   j 502 ÷ 100   k 9 ÷ 100   l 0·78 × 100

5. Rainbow Art pencils are sold in packs of 10 for £4·80 or in boxes of 100 for £39.

   a What is the cost of 1 pencil on the:
      i pack of 10   ii box of 100 offer?

   b The length of each pencil is 18·5 cm.
      Calculate the total length of 100 pencils laid end
      to end in a line on the gym hall floor.

6. One bottle of Citrus Twist drink has a volume of 2·25 litres.

   a What is the volume of:
      i 3 bottles   ii 5 bottles   iii 8 bottles?

   b One bottle normally costs £1·79, but a multipack
      of 6 bottles costs £9·18.

      How much is the cost **per bottle** if you buy the
      multipack?

7. a Seven boxes of bananas weigh a total of 86·52 kg.
      What is the weight of one box?
   b A 5 kg bag of new potatoes costs £7·30.
      An 8 kg bag costs £10·08.
      Which is the better buy?

8. a Martin saved up to buy a pair of jeans costing £38·78.
      He paid the exact amount using the fewest possible notes and coins.
      Write down the notes and coins he used.
   b Rachel bought a pair of jeans from the same shop for £35·29.
      She paid with two £20 notes.
      Write down the coins she was given in change.

2 Rounding to 1 Decimal Place

5·374

Rule for rounding

Examine the digit in the **second** decimal place.
If it's 5 or more   **round up**
If it's less than 5   **round down**
5·374 = 5·4 to 1 decimal place

A

1. Round each of these numbers to 1 decimal place:

   a 4·16   **b** 20·21   **c** 0·135   **d** 34·44
   e 78·05   **f** 67·94   **g** 0·996

2. In a swimming race, the top five times were recorded.
   Round each swimmer's time to 1 decimal place.

David	45.93 s
Zahid	42.56 s
Katie	43.44 s
Fiona	46.29 s
James	49.95 s

3.

> **The inch is an old-fashioned unit of measurement about the width of a thumb.**
>
> **1 inch = 2·54 cm**

   a Change the following into centimetres:
   i 3 inches   **ii** 6 inches   **iii** 9 inches

   b Round each answer to 1 decimal place.

4. Calculate the following, then round each answer to 1 decimal place:

   a 13·82 + 19·71   **b** 56·98 + 9·01   **c** 45·56 − 27·67
   d 23 − 18·45   **e** 34·08 + 20·96   **f** 80 − 21·05

5. Round each term to 1 decimal place to help you estimate the answer to the calculation.

   Example   4·453 + 2·316 is about 4·5 + 2·3, which is 6·8.

   a 7·545 + 2·192   **b** 15·674 + 7·242   **c** 12·786 − 5·468
   d 23·859 − 8·571   **e** 23·267 + 7·845   **f** 27·678 − 9·309

6. **a** Round the weight of each dog to 1 decimal place.
   b Estimate the difference in weight between:
   i the dalmatian and West Highland terrier
   ii the labrador and dalmatian
   iii the West Highland terrier and the labrador.

Dalmatian
24·652 kg

West Highland Terrier
10·142 kg

Labrador
29·888 kg

Challenge

A DIY store cut pieces of wood into the following lengths for a customer:

3·27 m	4·64 m	4·03 m
3·41 m	2·96 m	4·35 m

Which four pieces of wood have a length of **about** 15 m?

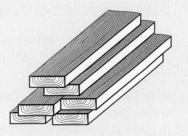

3 Multiplying and Dividing by 10, 100 and 1000

 A

1. Work out the following:

   a 11·56 × 10 b 32·67 × 100 c 2·25 × 1000
   d 7·1 ÷ 100 e 0·02 ÷ 10 f 0·263 × 1000
   g 23 ÷ 1000 h 20·06 × 1000 i 300·6 ÷ 100
   j 10·03 × 10 k 563 ÷ 1000 l 1·089 × 1000
   m 300·9 ÷ 100 n 50·4 × 1000 o 73·5 ÷ 1000

2.
   > 1 cm = 10 mm   1 m = 100 cm   1 km = 1000 m

   Copy and complete:

   a 33·7 cm = __ mm b 14·78 m = __ cm c 2·067 km = __ m
   d 50·6 mm = __ cm e 501·3 cm = __ m f 340·1 m = __ km
   g 0·085 km = __ m h 31 mm = __ m

3.
   > 1000 g = 1 kg   1000 kg = 1 tonne

   Copy and complete:

   a 7·6 kg = __ g b 4·92 tonnes = __ kg c 3·054 kg = __ g
   d 7142·6 g = __ kg e 6100·0 kg = __ tonnes f 1 tonne = __ g

4.

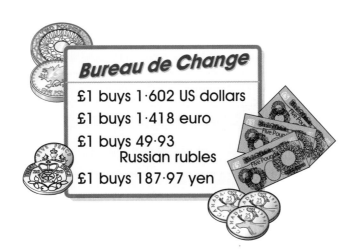

Bureau de Change

£1 buys 1·602 US dollars

£1 buys 1·418 euro

£1 buys 49·93 Russian rubles

£1 buys 187·97 yen

a Harry sent £10 in a birthday card to his French pen pal.
How many euro is this?

b How many Russian rubles can you get for £100?

c A family of 6 booked a holiday in Florida for £1000.
How many dollars is this?

d Jane had £100 worth of yen left from her holiday in Japan.
How many yen did she have?

e On a trip to Sydney, the Mackie family exchanged £1000 for 2393
Australian dollars. How many Australian dollars was £1 worth?

5. Gina buys a litre of gloss paint for £12.

Calculate the cost of 1 ml of paint in pence.

6. A stationery shop sells pencil sharpeners in boxes of 100.
They make a profit of 11·5p on every sharpener.

a How much profit do they make by selling:
  i 100 sharpeners?   ii 1000 sharpeners?

b Give your answers to i and ii in pounds.

c The shop makes a profit of £124·50 for selling 1000 biros.
How many pence profit is made on each pen sold?

Challenge

Calculate:

a (3·3 × 10) ÷ 100   b (10·2 ÷ 100) × 1000

c (235·6 ÷ 100) × 10   d ((1·89 × 1000) × 10) ÷ 100

e ((96 ÷ 1000) ÷ 10) × 100

4 Multiplying and Dividing a Decimal by a Whole Number

> When multiplying or dividing a decimal by a whole number **keep the decimal points in line**.

A

1. Calculate:

   a 23.7×4 b 107.5×6 c 32.07×9 d 53.77×4 e 20.33×5
   f 17.89×8 g 45.9×9 h 50.3×8 i 35.99×6 j 94.89×7

2. Find the answer:

   a $36.15 \div 3$ b $42.56 \div 4$ c $453.6 \div 6$ d $120.5 \div 5$ e $43.68 \div 7$
   f $40.44 \div 6$ g $80.99 \div 7$ h $71.37 \div 9$ i $91.7 \div 5$ j $75.6 \div 8$

3. A garden centre sells decorative gnome statues.

   a Mr Thrower bought four for his garden.
   Calculate the total weight of the statues.

   b Mrs Green bought six smaller gnome statues all the same weight.
   They weighed 58·5 kg in total.
   What was the weight of one statue?

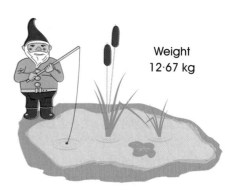

Weight
12·67 kg

4. A 4-pack of River Spring mineral water has a total volume of 11·16 litres.
   What is the volume of one bottle?

5. Suzi made eight payments of £13·50 for a school trip to Blair Darroch outdoor centre. How much did the trip cost her altogether?

6. Here are the temperatures in Edinburgh for five days in July:

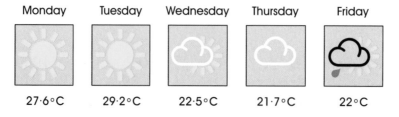

Monday	Tuesday	Wednesday	Thursday	Friday
27·6°C	29·2°C	22·5°C	21·7°C	22°C

Calculate the mean temperature over the five days.

Hint Find the total and divide by the number of readings.

7. Raja's piano lessons cost £11·75 each.

   a How much would he pay for five lessons?
   b A block of eight flute lessons costs £74. What is the cost of one lesson?

8. a Cheryl's gran works Monday to Saturday.
   She travels to work and back a total of 23·67 km each day.
   i How far does she travel in a week between work and home?
   ii Round your answer to 1 decimal place.

   b Cheryl's grandpa works a day less than her gran and travels 166 km in total per week. How far does he travel in one day?

9. a Lisa bought a mobile phone cover in France for €12·51.
   She worked out that this was exactly £9.
   How many euro did she get for £1?
   b Her brother Darryl spent £7 on a cap.
   How many euro was this?

10. a Greg came home from a holiday in Orlando with 14·58 US dollars ($) which he exchanged for £9.
    How much was £1 worth in dollars?
    b His friend Mark had five pounds worth of US dollars left.
    How many dollars did he have?

11. Caledonian College offers a range of Saturday clubs.

    a Calculate the cost per week for:
       i basketball coaching
       ii art classes
       iii football coaching
       iv drama classes.

    b The cost of the computer club was £4·75 per week.
    Hannah went for six weeks.
    How much did she pay?

Saturday Clubs

Basketball £41·70 (6 weeks)
Art £58·32 (8 weeks)
Football £34·45 (5 weeks)
Drama £47·25 (9 weeks)

Challenge

Simon booked a set of six badminton classes for £44·94.
Karen booked eight netball classes.
Each netball lesson cost a seventh less than a badminton lesson.

How much did Karen pay for her eight netball lessons?

Investigate

1. Which of these numbers multiplied by 7 gives a total of 612·36?

88·88
87·48   85·98
86·28 89·58

2. Which of these numbers divided by 6 and then multiplied by 9 gives the total 128·97?

B

1. Calculate:

    a   68·78 × 6   b   95·06 × 9   c   325 ÷ 4   d   461·1 ÷ 5
    e   7·782 × 8   f   5·909 × 7   g   8·208 ÷ 8   h   3·312 ÷ 9
    i   (124 ÷ 8) × 9   j   (1·236 × 7) ÷ 4

2. a   Mr and Mrs Chakravarti and their two children plan a holiday to Greece.
      i   Which travel firm offers the best deal?
      ii   How much cheaper is it?

   b   A group of four adults and six children want to book a week in Spain.
      i   Which travel firm offers the best deal?
      ii   How much cheaper Is It?

Sun Savers

2 weeks in Greece
Adults £275·89
Children £145·65

1 week in Spain
Adults £199·75
Children £104·99

Happy Holidays

2 weeks in Greece
Adults £290·25
Children £123·95

1 week in Spain
Adults £187·99
Children £112·50

3. A delivery van holds six packages each weighing 78·89 kg and nine each weighing 50·78 kg.

   a   What is the total weight of all of the packages?
   b   Round your answer to 1 decimal place.

4. Returning home from Europe, a group of friends compared how much money they had left. Jane had £6 worth of euro left, Mike had £8 worth, Sameera had £4 worth and Eddie had £9 worth.
   If £1 = €1·44, calculate the mean amount of euro they had left.

   Hint First work out the mean amount of pounds they had.

5. On a trip to Florida, the Cooper family spent $481·25 in a week.

   a How much on average did they spend in one day?
   b For £5, they could get $8·11. How much was £1 worth?

6. Coffee.Com, an Internet cafe, ordered eight pints of milk from their suppliers. This is equal to 14·072 litres.

   a How many pints are in one litre?
   b Round your answer to 1 decimal place.

Challenge

Calculate the area of the garden pool.

Remember
Area = length ×
breadth

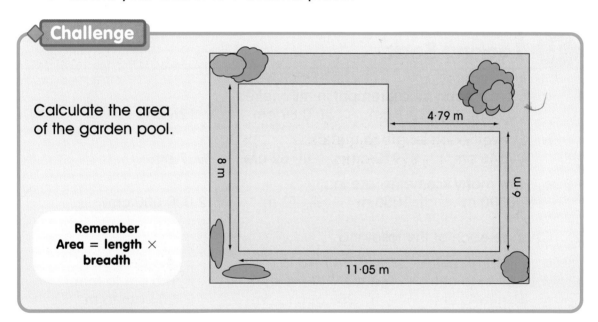

Investigate

Each star represents a digit, but not necessarily the same digit.

Find the value of each star.

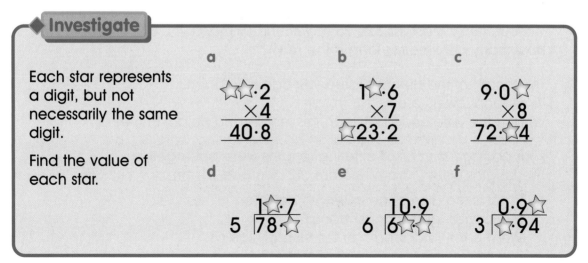

Unit 12 Length

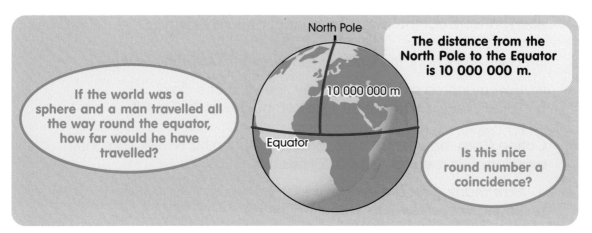

If the world was a sphere and a man travelled all the way round the equator, how far would he have travelled?

The distance from the North Pole to the Equator is 10 000 000 m.

10 000 000 m

North Pole

Equator

Is this nice round number a coincidence?

1 Looking Back

1. a Express each measurement in millimetres:
   i 35 cm   ii 2·7 cm   iii 0·89 cm   iv 126 cm

   b Convert each length to metres:
   i 7546 cm   ii 912 cm   iii 62 cm   iv 7 cm

   c How many kilometres are in:
   i 8500 m   ii 1050 m   iii 77 m   iv 2 000 000 cm?

2. Change each of the following:

a 17 km to metres	b 7·43 km to metres	c 4·3 m to cm
d 0·09 m to cm	e 297 cm to mm	f 0·5 cm to mm
g 41 mm to cm	h 758 mm to cm	i 204 cm to m

3. The height of the Eiffel Tower is given in the record books as 300·5 m without the TV mast, or 320·75 m with the TV mast.
   How many centimetres long is the mast?

4. The length of the Humber Estuary Bridge is 1·41 km.
   Its support towers are 162·5 m tall.
   What is the difference between this length and height in metres?

5. Four postage stamps of differing lengths were put together.
   The lengths were 2·3 cm, 3·6 cm, 42 mm and 51 mm.

   a What is the difference in length between the longest and shortest stamp?

   b What is the total length of the strip of stamps:
   i in millimetres   ii in centimetres?

6. In this drawing, 2 centimetres represents 1 metre.

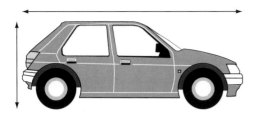

By measuring to the nearest millimetre, calculate:

a the length of the car
b the height of the car
c the height of a window
d the diameter of a tyre.

2 Measurements in Calculations

When using measurements in calculations:

❖ always work in a single unit
❖ always quote the units of the answer.

 A

1. To open the school sports, eight relay runners carry a baton a total distance of 1 kilometre.

   What distance does each person run if they all run the same amount?

2. Carron Primary School decided to collect a kilometre of 20p pieces for charity.

   One 20p piece has a diameter of 22 mm.

   a i How many coins must be collected to get just over a metre?
      ii What actual distance is covered by this amount of coins.

   b i How many coins must be collected to get just over a kilometre?
      ii With this number of coins, how much more than a kilometre do they have?

3. The perimeter is the total distance round a shape.

    a   What is the perimeter of each rectangle below:

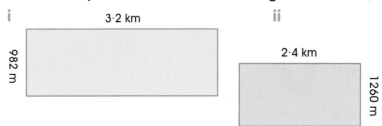

    i   3·2 km   982 m

    ii   2·4 km   1260 m

    b   A square of side 2091 m will have the same perimeter as the first rectangle. Check whether this is true.
    c   What will the side of a square measure, if it has the same perimeter as the second rectangle?

4. In October 1990, Lin Youdian walked the entire length of the Great Wall of China.

    This wall has a main length of 3460 km and an additional length of 2860 km made up of various branches.

    a   What is the total length of the wall?
    b   It took Lin 2 years to walk the wall.

    At 365 days to a year, what distance was he averaging a day (to the nearest metre)?

5. The car ferry has a bay of length 28 m in which it can hold vehicles.
    There is enough room in the bay for two lanes.
    Suppose the average length of a vehicle is 380 cm.

    a   How many cars can it carry, bumper-to-bumper, in the bay?
    b   The fare for one car is £72·20.
        How much are they charging per centimetre?

B

1. The distance between Ian's house and his school was 894 m.

    a   How many kilometres did he walk going to and from school each day assuming he walked home for lunch?
    b   A school year is 195 days long. How far did he walk to and from school in a year if he had no absences?
    c   How many years would he need to attend school before he has done the equivalent of a walk from the North Pole to the Equator?

2. How thick is one sheet of paper if 500 sheets form a pile 5 cm thick?

3. An article on the growth of motorways showed the following table:

Year	1958	1971	1977	1978
Motorways in use (km)	nil	1270	2290	2416

The first motorway was begun in 1958.

a How many kilometres of motorway had been built by 1971?
b Assuming 1958 to 1971 is 13 years of building, what is the mean length of road built per year in this period (to the nearest 100 m)?
c i How many kilometres of motorway were built between 1971 and 1977?
  ii Calculate the mean length of road built per year in this period.

d How does the motorway building between 1977 and 1978 compare with that of 1971 to 1977?

3 Drawing Simple Shapes

When drawing shapes, always make a rough sketch, with sizes shown, to help you plan the accurate drawing.

A sharp pencil will help your accuracy

A

1. Make accurate drawings of each of the following rectangles and then measure the diagonals correct to the nearest millimetre.

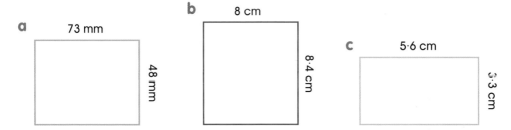

a 73 mm   48 mm
b 8 cm   8·4 cm
c 5·6 cm   3·3 cm

2. a Make an accurate drawing of rectangles with the following dimensions:
   i 65 mm × 72 mm   ii 60 mm × 68 mm   iii 9·0 cm × 5·6 cm.

b Measure the length of the diagonals.
c Measure the size of the acute angle made between the diagonals.

A right-angled triangle is half of a rectangle.

3. a Make an accurate drawing of the right-angled triangle where the sides forming the right angle are of length 6·0 cm by 3·2 cm.
   b Measure the length of the third side.

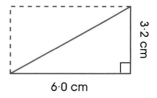

3·2 cm

6·0 cm

4. a Draw right-angled triangles where the sides forming the right angle are of length:
   i 77 mm by 36 mm   ii 96 mm by 40 mm   iii 8·4 cm by 8·8 cm.

   b For each triangle, measure:
   i the length of the third side   ii the size of each angle.

5. a To draw the shape shown:
   i Draw a line 7·5 cm long.
   ii Draw the 4·5 cm and 8·5 cm lines at right angles to the 7·5 cm line.
   iii Join the ends of these lines to form the quadrilateral.

   b Measure the length of the fourth side.
   c Calculate the perimeter of the shape.
   d i Measure the size of each angle.
     ii What is the sum of all four angles?

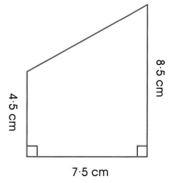

8·5 cm

4·5 cm

7·5 cm

6. The diagram shows a sketch of a symmetrical pentagon.

   a Follow these instructions to make an accurate drawing of the pentagon:
   i Draw the base line.
   ii Draw the three vertical lines.
   iii Join the tops of the vertical lines to complete the shape.

   b Measure the lengths of the missing sides.
   c Calculate the perimeter of the pentagon.

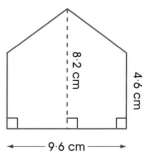

8·2 cm

4·6 cm

9·6 cm

Challenge

Three balls rest against the cushion as shown.
What is the distance x if a ball has a radius of 3 cm?
Finding out how to draw the three circles is part of the puzzle.

x

Using Scale Drawings

The above exercise shows us that drawings can help us find sizes that are not already measured. Sometimes, however, the real shape is too big to draw. We then have to make use of scale drawings.

> **Always state the scale on the drawing.**

One form in which the scale can be given is called the **representative fraction**.

A scale where 1 centimetre represents a metre can be written as **1 cm:1 m** and then simplified.

	1 cm:1 m
First, get the units the same on both sides:	= 1 cm:100 cm
Once the units are the same, they are no longer required.	= 1:100

1:100 doesn't just tell you that 1 cm represents 100 cm. It also tells you that 1 mm represents 100 mm, and that 3 cm represents 3×100 cm = 300 cm, and so on.

Example   Express a scale where 1 cm represents 5 km as a representative fraction.

$$1 \text{ cm:5 km}$$
$$= 1 \text{ cm:5000 m}$$
$$= 1 \text{ cm:500 000 cm}$$
$$= 1:500\ 000$$

1. Write the following scales as representative fractions:

   a 1 cm represents 10 m   b 1 mm represents 10 cm
   c 1 cm represents 1 km   d 1 cm represents 25 m
   e 1 mm represents 20 m   f 1 mm represents 50 km
   g 1 mm represents 2 cm   h 1 cm represents 100 km
   i   2 mm represents 50 km

2. Where the scale is 1:50, what length is represented by:

   a 1 cm   b 1 mm   c 3 cm   d 3 mm
   e 7 cm   f 12 mm   g 23 cm   h 45·2 cm?

3. Where the scale is 1:200, what length, in metres, is represented by:

   a 1 cm   **b** 3 cm   **c** 3·6 cm   **d** 5 mm
   e 75 cm   **f** 35 mm   **g** 36 cm   **h** 12·3 cm?

4. A map is drawn to a scale of 1:5000.

   a What does 1 cm represent in metres, on this scale?
   b On the map, two houses are separated by a distance of 7·5 cm. How far apart are they in real life?
   c A field is rectangular. On the map, it is 4 cm by 5 cm.
       i What are its real dimensions?
       ii What is its perimeter?

   d Make an accurate scale drawing of the field and figure out the actual length of its diagonals.

5. **a** When the scale is 1:200, we multiply scaled lengths by 200 to find the actual sizes. What do we do if we have actual sizes and wish to turn them into scaled lengths?
   b What would be the scaled length which represents an actual size of:
       i 800 cm   **ii** 2000 cm   **iii** 20 m
       iv 65 m   **v** 5 m   **vi** 80 cm?

   Hint Be careful with the units!

6. This is a plan of Margaret's bedroom.
   It is drawn to the scale 1:50.

   a What is the length of:
       i the bed
       ii the bookshelf?

   b What are the dimensions of:
       i the room
       ii the computer desk?

   c How wide is the actual door?

   d Meg would like to include a circular table of diameter 80 cm. What size will this be on the plan?

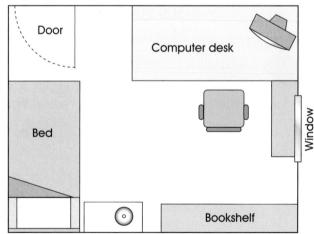

Scale 1:50

   e The overhead light is located right above the spot where the diagonals cross. How far from the corner of the room is this spot?

Enlarging

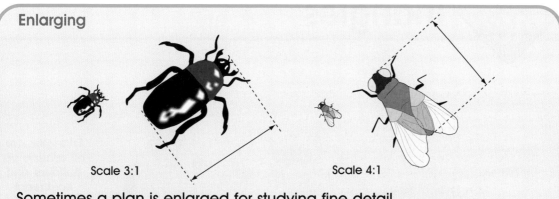

Scale 3:1   Scale 4:1

Sometimes a plan is enlarged for studying fine detail.
In these pictures, the beetle has been enlarged three times,
so the scale is written **3:1**.
The fly has been enlarged by a scale of **4:1**.

B

1. **a** **i** What size is the enlarged beetle?
   ii Calculate the size of the actual beetle.

   b What is the actual length of the beetle's:
   i feeler   **ii** hindmost leg?

   c How long is the fly's body?
   d How wide is the fly from wing tip to wing tip?

2. A small model of a bus is made by gluing pictures onto a cuboid.
   The cuboid is 3 cm long by 1·5 cm high by 1·1 cm wide.
   The actual bus is 6 m high.

   a Calculate the scale of the model.
   b What actual distance is
   represented by:
   i 3 cm   **ii** 1·1 cm?

   c Construct such a model.

3. The cyclist has been modelled by the triangular prism shown.
   The height of the triangle, from the base to the point above the cyclist's
   head, represents 2 m.

   a Measure this distance in millimetres.
   b Calculate the scale of the model.
   c What is the diameter of an actual wheel?
   d What is the height from the ground to the crossbar of
   the bike?
   e Try making a model similar to this.
   f Could the bus above and the cyclist be in the same
   model village? Give a reason for your answer.

Unit 13 Triangles

Triangles are all around us. Builders and engineers have used them for centuries to strengthen and balance structures.

1 Looking Back

An equilateral triangle has three axes of symmetry.

An isosceles triangle has one axis of symmetry.

A right-angled triangle has one right angle.

1. The artist has drawn two equilateral triangles, two isosceles triangles, two right-angled triangles and one other. He has forgotten to label which is which. Use a ruler and protractor to help you decide.

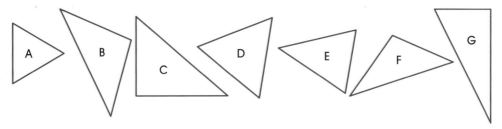

2. All the angles of an equilateral triangle are the same size.
   We know they add up to 180°.
   What size is each angle?

3. △ ABC is isosceles. ∠ABC = 50°.

   a What size is ∠ACB? Give a reason.
   b What size is ∠CAB? Give a reason.

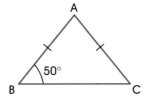

A triangle that contains an obtuse angle is called an obtuse-angled triangle. If a triangle has neither an obtuse angle nor a right angle, it is called an acute-angled triangle.

4. For each triangle below:

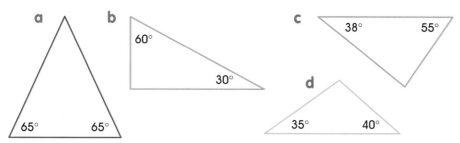

      i calculate the missing angle   ii decide which type of triangle it is.

5. Copy the diagrams and fill in the size of each angle:

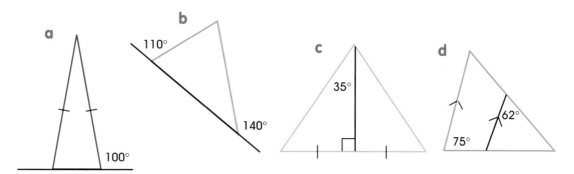

 Drawing Triangles 1

A

1. Make an accurate drawing of each sketch with the help of a ruler and a set of compasses:

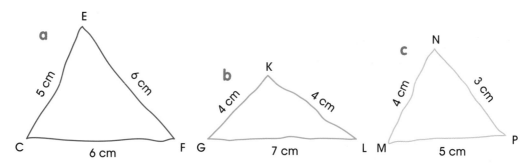

2. Draw each of the following triangles:

   a △ ABC where
      AB = 6 cm, BC = 6·5 cm and CA = 7 cm
   b △ PQR where
      PQ = 5 cm, QR = 12 cm and RP = 13 cm
   c △ PRS where
      PR = RS = 8 cm and SP = 4 cm

3. An equilateral triangle has a side of length 7 cm.

   a Make an accurate drawing of the triangle.
   b Draw the lines of symmetry on your diagram.
   c Mark in the size of each angle.

4. △ XYZ is an isosceles triangle. XY = 4 cm and YZ = 6 cm.

   a There are two triangles that fit this description.
      Draw them both.
   b Measure the angles in both triangles.

5. Peter said he could draw a triangle with sides of 3 cm, 4 cm and 8 cm.

   a Try to draw the triangle starting by drawing the 8 cm line.
   b What do you notice?
   c Which of the following sets of lengths could not be used to draw a triangle:

      i   4 cm, 5 cm, 9 cm
      ii 6 cm, 12 cm, 5 cm
      iii 6 cm, 4·5 cm, 3·7 cm
      iv 8·2 cm, 4·1 cm, 3·9 cm

6.

Triangle							Angle Sum
ABC	AB	6 cm	AC	5 cm	BC	7 cm	
DEF	DE	7 cm	DF	4 cm	EF	8 cm	
GHI	GH	55 mm	GI	65 mm	HI	75 mm	
JKL	JK	35 mm	JL	42 mm	KL	58 mm	

   a Draw the triangles described in the table
   b Check that in each case the angle sum is 180°.

B

Using Scale Drawings

1. A yacht sailed in a straight line from Ardbay to Broadloch, a distance of 6 km. It sails passed a lighthouse that is 4 km from Ardbay and 3 km from Broadloch.
   How close does it get to the lighthouse?

   a Draw a triangle of sides 6 cm, 3 cm and 4 cm to represent the situation. This uses a scale of 1 cm:1 km.
   b Measure the distance on your drawing as indicated in this sketch:
   c Scale this length up to find the closest the yacht got to the lighthouse.

2. A balloon is tethered to the ground.
   The tethers are 55 m and 45 m long as shown.
   They are fixed to the ground 35 m apart.

   a Using a scale of 1 mm:1 m draw a triangle to represent the situation.
   b What angle does each tether make with the ground?
   c What is the vertical height of the balloon (marked in red in the sketch).

3. At the school concert, a spotlight is aimed at the stage.
   It makes a spot of length 5 m as shown.
   Other measurements are shown in the diagram.

   a Make an accurate scale drawing of the triangle representing the beam of light. Use a scale of 1 cm:2 m.
   b Measure the angle that the beam of light spreads out.
   c How high above the stage is the spotlight (the height marked in red)?

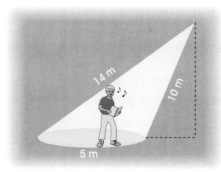

3 ▶ Drawing Triangles 2

Example   Draw triangle ABC with sides AB = 5 cm, BC = 6 cm and ∠ABC = 40°.

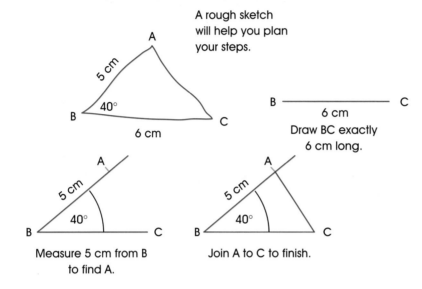

A rough sketch will help you plan your steps.

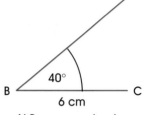

Draw BC exactly 6 cm long.

At B, use a protractor to measure and draw a 40° angle.

Measure 5 cm from B to find A.

Join A to C to finish.

 A

1. Make an accurate drawing of each sketch with the help of a ruler and a protractor:

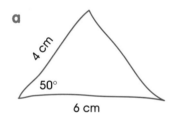   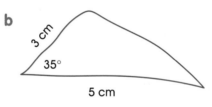   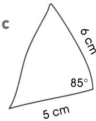

2. Draw each of the following triangles:

   a   △ ABC where AB = 5 cm, BC = 4 cm, ∠ABC = 55°
   b   △ PQR where PQ = 6 cm, QR = 8 cm, ∠PQR = 80°

3. a   Make an accurate drawing of an equilateral triangle by measuring two sides and the angle between them.
      The sides of the triangle have to be 5 cm long.
   b   Measure the third side to check it is the same length as the others.

4.   △ XYZ has sides XY = 5 cm and YZ = 5·5 cm.
     The angle between these sides is 30°.

     a   Make an accurate drawing of the triangle.
     b   i   What are the sizes of the other angles?
         ii   What is the length of ZX?

B

Using Scale Drawings

1. Two ships, the *Abigale* and the *Blyth Spirit*, leave the same port. They both go in straight lines. Their routes are 25° apart. The *Abigale* sails 8 km and in the same time the *Blyth Spirit* travels 7 km.

   a Draw an accurate triangle to represent the situation. Use a scale of 1 cm:1 km. Label the vertices P, A and B.
   b How far apart are the *Abigale* and the *Blyth Spirit*? Measure AB and scale up.

2. Sean was at the famous Queen's View. A plaque told him the distance to various landmarks. The church tower was 1 km away. The Black Crag was 2 km away. Sean measured the angle between these directions as 30°.

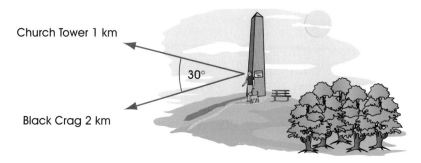

Church Tower 1 km

30°

Black Crag 2 km

   a Using a scale of 1:200, make an accurate drawing of the triangle that represents this situation.
   b How far apart are the tower and the Black Crag?

3. Helen watched a plane taking off.

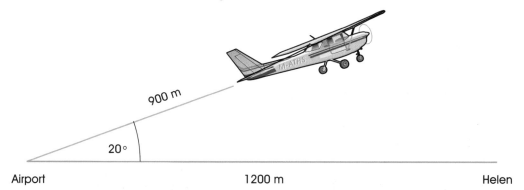

900 m

20°

Airport   1200 m   Helen

   a Make a scale drawing of the situation as shown above.
   b How far apart are the plane and Helen at this point?
   c How far apart will they be when the plane has travelled:
      i another 100 m   ii another 900 m?

4 Drawing Triangles 3

1. a   Follow these steps to draw the triangle:
       i   Draw AC 5 cm long.
       ii   Draw AB so that ∠CAB = 40°.
       iii Draw BC so that ∠ACB = 50°.
       iv   Where these lines cross is the point B.
            Complete the triangle ABC.

    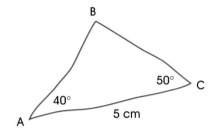

    b   i   What is the size of the third angle?
            Do you need the drawing for this?
       ii   What is the lengths of the other two sides?
       iii What is the perimeter of the triangle?

2. Draw each of the following triangles:

    a   △ ABC where AB = 5 cm, ∠BAC = 55°, ∠ABC = 40°.
    b   △ PQR where PQ = 6 cm, ∠QPR = 45°, ∠PQR = 65°.
    c   △ PRS where PR = 7 cm, ∠PRS = ∠RPS = 50°.

3. a   Draw an equilateral triangle of side 6 cm by measuring one side and
        two angles only.
    b   Check that the other sides and angles are what they should be.

4. △ ABC has side AB = 6 cm. The angle at A = 40°. The angle at B = 120°.

    a   Make an accurate drawing of triangle ABC.
    b   i   What size should the third angle be?
       ii   Measure to check this.
    c   i   Measure the length of the other sides.
       ii   What is the perimeter of the shape?

◆ **Investigate**

Geoff said that the longest side of a triangle is always opposite the
biggest angle. George wasn't sure.

   a   Is Geoff correct?
   b   Is a similar statement true about:
       i the smallest angle   ii the middle-sized angle?

Draw some triangles and explore the situation!

Using Scale Drawings

1. Deirdre stands 9 metres away from the base of a tree.
   She had to look up through an angle of 45° to see the tree top.
   Assume the tree makes a right angle with the ground.

   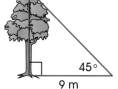

   a Draw a triangle to represent the situation.
      Represent the tree by a straight line and use
      a scale of 1:100.
   b How high is the tree?

2. Terri stands 12 metres from another tree.
   She had to look up through 30° to see the top of the tree.

   a Make a scale drawing, assuming the tree makes
      an angle of 90° with the ground.
   b What is the height of the tree?
   c How far is it from Terri to the top of the tree?

3. Jackie and Lydia want to find out how wide the river is.
   They place two markers 20 m apart on their
   bank of the river.

   They fix on a tree (T) on the opposite bank.
   They measure some angles as shown.

   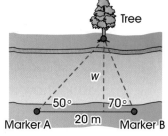

   a Make a scale drawing of the triangle ABT.
   b i Measure w on your scale drawing.
      ii Scale it up to find the width of the river.

4. Caroline and Dafydd are 100 m apart.
   Above and between them they spot a glider.
   Caroline has to look up through an angle of 80° to look at it.
   David has to look through an angle of 85°.
   Use a scale drawing to figure out how high the glider is.

   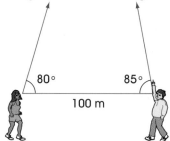

Unit 14 Area

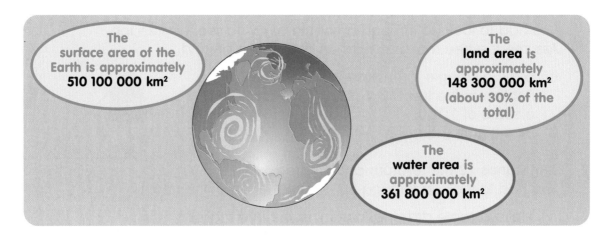

The surface area of the Earth is approximately **510 100 000 km²**

The **land area is** approximately **148 300 000 km²** (about 30% of the total)

The **water area is** approximately **361 800 000 km²**

1 Looking Back

1. Imagine a square centimetre grid placed on top of each rectangle.

   For each rectangle:
   - i   count how many squares are in each row
   - ii count how many rows there are
   - iii calculate the area.

   a   3 cm   4 cm

   b   3 cm   3 cm

   c   2 cm   6 cm

   d   5 cm   3 cm

2.

A children's playground is rectangular.
It is 20 m long and 18 m broad.
The playground needs to be tiled with square rubber tiles of side 1 metre.

a   How many tiles are needed?
b   What is the area of the playground?

3. Calculate the area of triangle ABC. Each square represents 1 cm².

4.

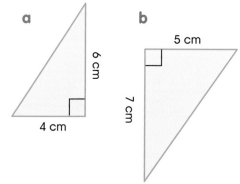

a

b
5 cm

c
13 cm

5 cm

12 cm

i Draw each of these right-angled triangles on centimetre squared paper.
ii Calculate the area of each triangle.

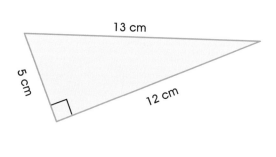

5. a Draw the triangular roof on squared paper. Use 1 square to represent 1 m².
   b Find the area of the roof.

6. The trapezium has been made from two right-angled triangles and a rectangle. Each square represents 1 cm².

Find the area of the trapezium.

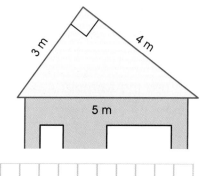

7. a How many millimetres in 1 centimetre?
   b How many mm² in 1 cm²?
   c Change to mm²: i 6 cm²   ii 9·5 cm²
   d Change to cm²: i 900 mm²   ii 1750 mm²

8. Estimate these areas in mm²:

   a Your thumb nail
   b The end of your pencil
   c The surface of one side of a 5p coin
   d This bumble bee

2 The Area of a Rectangle

| Area = length × breadth | For a rectangle: | $A = lb$ | For a square: | $A = l^2$ |

A

1. Use the formula $A = lb$ to help you calculate the area of each rectangle:

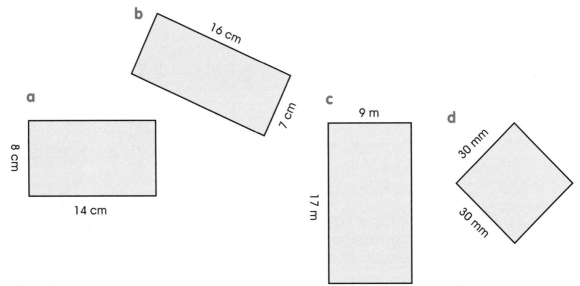

b
16 cm
7 cm

a
8 cm
14 cm

c
9 m
17 m

d
30 mm
30 mm

2. Use the formula $A = l^2$ to help you calculate the area of each square:

a
8 cm

b
70 mm

c
90 cm

3. Calculate the area of each rectangle and square:

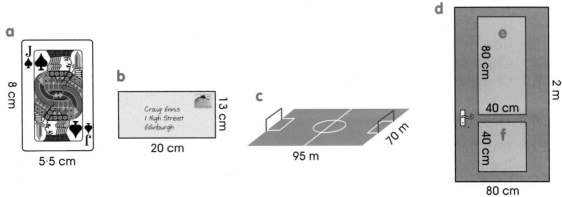

a
8 cm
5·5 cm

b
Craig Ennis
1 High Street
Edinburgh
20 cm
13 cm

c
95 m
70 m

d
e
80 cm
40 cm
2 m
f
40 cm
80 cm

Hint Be careful with units.

4. Find the area of:

   a the left side of the filing cabinet
   b its front
   c its top.

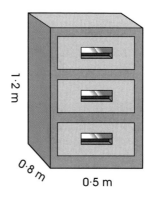

1·2 m

0·8 m   0·5 m

5. The painting has a uniform border
   of 7 cm surrounding it.
   Calculate:

   a the dimensions of the painting
   b the area of the painting.

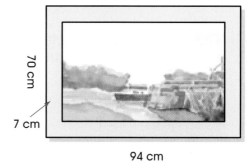

70 cm

7 cm

94 cm

6. The diagram shows the plan for a
   rectangular children's playground.
   Rectangular areas for swings, a
   chute and a climbing frame are
   set into the grass playground.
   All measurements are in metres.

   a Calculate the area of the
     playground.
   b Calculate the area of:
     i   the swings
     ii the chute
     iii the climbing frame.
   c What area of the playground is grass?

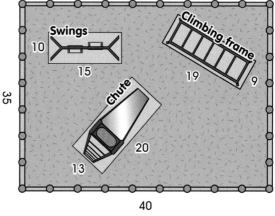

Swings
10
15
Climbing frame
19   9
35
Chute
20
13
40

B

1. Calculate the area of each shape by first breaking it up into rectangles.
   All measurements are in centimetres.

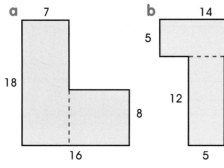

a   7

18

16

b   14

5

12

8

5

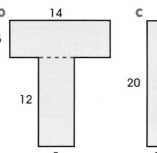

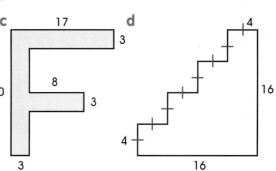

c   17

3

20   8

3

3

d   4

16

4

16

The areas of some shapes can be calculated by considering the surrounding rectangle.

2. a What is the area of the rectangle surrounding the coloured shape?
   b Calculate the areas of rectangles A, B and C.
   c What is the area of the coloured shape?

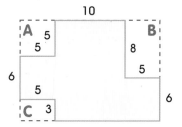

3. Calculate the areas of these shapes by considering the surrounding rectangles (all measurements are in centimetres).

a

b

c

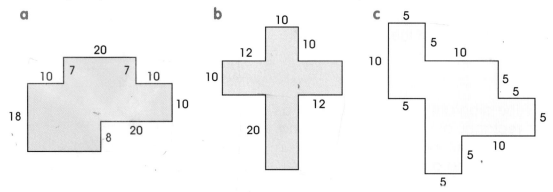

4. A plan of the Ace Leisure Centre is shown.
   It sits in rectangular grounds, which have been surfaced with tar, and is made up of a number of rectangular buildings.

   a Calculate the area of:
      i   the swimming pool
      ii   the games hall
      iii the library.

   b Calculate the area of tar.

Plan of Ace Leisure Centre

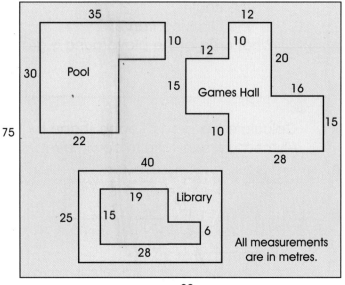

All measurements are in metres.

Challenge

A pattern is made from four squares.
The squares have sides of length 1 cm, 3 cm, 5 cm
and 7 cm.

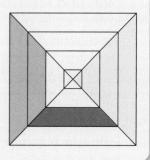

a Calculate the shaded area on
the right-hand side.
b Calculate the shaded area on the left-hand side.
c Calculate the other shaded area.

3 Estimate Areas in Square Metres

To estimate the area of a rectangle:
estimate its **length**, estimate its **breadth** and **multiply**.

1. a Estimate the length and breadth of the classroom door.
    b Use these estimates to write down an estimate in m^2 for the area
       of the classroom door.

2. Repeat question **1** for:
    i   the blackboard   ii   the classroom floor (if it is a rectangle)
    iii the classroom ceiling   iv   the dining hall floor.

3. Check your area answers to question **2** with those calculated from actual
    measurements.

4. Copy and complete a table like the one below. Include some other
    rectangular areas.

Item	Length (m) Estimate	Breadth (m) Estimate	Area (m²)	Length (m) Measurement	Breadth (m) Measurement	Area (m²)
Door						
Blackboard						
Floor						
Ceiling						
Dining hall floor						

5. The diagram shows the plan of a reservoir drawn to the scale of 1 cm represents 100 m. The plan is surrounded by a rectangle measuring 10 cm by 5 cm.

Estimate the area of the reservoir in square metres.

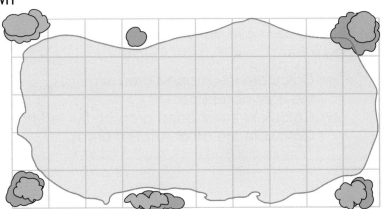

 4 Large Areas

Large areas are measured in **hectares (ha)**.

1 hectare = 100 m × 100 m

1 hectare = 10 000 m²

The area of a full-sized football pitch is just under 1 hectare.

Very large areas in **square kilometres (km²)**.

1 km² = 1000 m × 1000 m

So, 1 km² = 1 000 000 m²

The area of Scotland is approximately 79 000 km².

A

1. Change to hectares:

a 50 000 m²   b 90 000 m²   c 120 000 m²   d 75 000 m²
e 1 000 000 m² f 14 500 000 m² g 187 000 m²   h 4000 m²

2. Change to m²:

a 8 hectares   b 23 hectares   c 4·6 hectares   d 0·54 hectares

3. Change to km²:

   a 4 500 000 m² b 17 600 000 m² c 200 000 m² d 775 000 m²

4. a Work out the number of hectares in 1 km².
   b Change to km²:
      i   700 hectares   ii 1250 hectares
      iii 14 860 hectares   iv 35 hectares

   c Change to hectares:
      i   12 km²   ii 163 km²
      iii 3·25 km²   iv 0·8 km²

5. The area of Scotland is approximately 79 000 km².
   What is the area of Scotland in:

   a hectares (ha)
   b square metres (m²)?

6. Use the information given in the table to calculate the following:

   a The area of Arran in m².
   b The area of Great Britain in ha.
   c Approximately how many times bigger is:
      i   the State of Texas than Great Britain
      ii Africa than Europe
      iii Australia than Great Britain?

   d 1 km² = 0·3861 square miles.

   Calculate in square miles:
      i   the area of Scotland   ii the area of Canada.

Land Mass	Area (km²)
Arran	430
Scotland	79 000
Great Britain	224 800
Texas	691 003
Australia	7 692 300
Canada	9 971 500
Europe	10 245 000
Africa	30 970 000

Unit 15 — Whole Numbers

Numbers are everywhere you go

It is **300 m (984 feet)** high. Its base forms a square of side **126 m** **(414 feet)**

It is made from **15 000** separate iron parts, held together by **25 000 000** rivets

Gustave Eiffel (1832–1923) designed the Eiffel Tower in Paris. It was completed in 1889 and took over two years to build.

The total weight of these materials is **8219 tonnes**

1 Looking Back

1. Write these numbers in words:

   a 8 512 263   b 7 081 306   c 372 601 450

2. Write these numbers in figures:

   a *seventeen million, two hundred and forty-six thousand, three hundred and one*
   b *four million, eight thousand and sixty-seven*
   c *eight hundred and five million, one hundred and ninety thousand, six hundred and thirteen*

3. Consider the number **789 096**. Write down the number that is:

   a 100 more   b 1000 more   c 20 000 more   d 100 less.

4. Consider the number **6 029 153**. Write down the number that is:

   a 1000 more   b 200 less   c 100 000 less   d 90 000 more.

5. a Add 1 to 645 999.   b Subtract 1 from 1 010 000.
   c Subtract 1 from 17 909 000.   d Add 1 to 190 999 999.

6. Write these meter readings in order, starting with the largest:

a | 8 | 2 | 3 | 9 | 1 | 7 | b | 8 | 3 | 0 | 6 | 4 | 5 | c | 8 | 1 | 8 | 7 | 6 | 9 |

d | 8 | 1 | 6 | 9 | 9 | 5 | e | 8 | 2 | 5 | 6 | 1 | 0 |

7. Round:

   a 369 237 to the nearest 10   b 6 345 025 to the nearest 10
   c 706 183 to the nearest 100   d 6 186 037 to the nearest 100
   e 494 500 to the nearest 1000   f 18 376 497 to the nearest 1000.

8. Round these measurements to the nearest metre:

   a 8 metres 72 centimetres   b 17 metres 36 centimetres

9. Round to the nearest kilogram:

   a 14 kilograms 504 grams   b 6 kilograms 98 grams

10. Round to the nearest hour:

   a 7 hours 40 minutes   b 9 hours 35 minutes   c 16 hours 19 minutes

11. Calculate:

   a 724 × 30   b 3684 × 500   c 67 300 ÷ 50   d 275 800 000 ÷ 400

12. A prime number has only two factors: itself and 1.
    List all the prime numbers between 60 and 70.

13. List the factors of 54.

14. Which factors of 168 are prime?

B

1. Calculate:

   a   3865   b   9989   c   2135   d   5702   e   7000
        + 4768   + 9899   − 1687   − 2836   − 4138

   f 8567   g 6948   h 4445 ÷ 7   i 4698 ÷ 6   j 8802 ÷ 9
        × 9   × 8

b How many passengers were given a guided tour during:
   i February ii April iii July iv August
   v the last three months of the year?

c Assuming Maria's bus was full for every tour in October, how many tours of the city did she make?

 Around Europe with a Calculator

Remember to **estimate, calculate, check**.

1. Five of the largest capital cities in the European Union and their populations are given in the table:

Capital city	Athens	London	Madrid	Paris	Rome
Population	3 235 250	7 077 140	2 947 860	2 251 270	2 820 050

   a Calculate the total population of the five capitals.
   b How many more people live in London than in:
      i Athens ii Madrid iii Paris iv Rome?

2. The four busiest air routes within the EU last year involved flights to and from London. They were:

   Dublin/London with 4 345 310 passengers
   Amsterdam/London with 3 513 832 passengers
   London/Paris with 2 843 717 passengers
   Frankfurt/London with 2 017 405 passengers.

   a How many passengers altogether flew on these four routes?
   b How many more flew between Dublin and London than between Amsterdam and London?

3. The table shows the land areas of some countries in the EU.

Country	Austria	France	Germany	UK	Italy	L/bourg	Spain
Area (km²)	83 854	551 232	357 868	244 755	301 252	2586	504 723

   a What is the difference in area between:
      i the UK and France
      ii the UK and Austria
      iii Spain and Germany?

b   How many times bigger than Luxembourg is:
     i the UK   ii France   iii Austria   iv Italy?

     Give your answers correct to the nearest whole number.

c   Greece is approximately 51 times bigger than Luxembourg.
     Find the land area of Greece, to the nearest 100 km².

4.   A day ticket for a sunbed on an Italian beach costs €22.
     A weekly ticket costs €54.
     The table shows the number of each type of ticket bought
     each month last summer:

Month	May	Jun	Jul	Aug	Sep
No. of day tickets	7431	9247	13 746	16 824	11 386
No. of weekly tickets	5189	8613	10 163	12 035	9572

a   Calculate the amount of money spent each month on sunbeds.
b   How much money was spent altogether over the five months?

Challenge

1.   The pages of a book are numbered 1, 2, 3, 4, and so on. No pages
     are missing.

     The digit **3** occurs in the page numbers exactly 99 times.
     What is the number of the last page? Explain your answer.

2. $13 \times 24 + 5$ and $315 \times 4 + 2$ are two calculations involving each
     of the digits 1, 2, 3, 4 and 5 only once and each of the operations
     $\times$ and $+$ only once. The multiplication is carried out before the
     addition.

     Find the calculation of this kind that gives the largest possible value,
     and explain how you found it. You are allowed the help of a
     calculator.

3.   Use your calculator where necessary to help you determine which of
     these numbers are prime numbers:

     a 1   b 11   c 111   d 1111
     e 11 111   f 111 111   g 1 111 111   h 11 111 111
     i 111 111 111   j 1 111 111 111

Unit 16 Equations and Inequations

Equations crop up in the most unlikely situations!

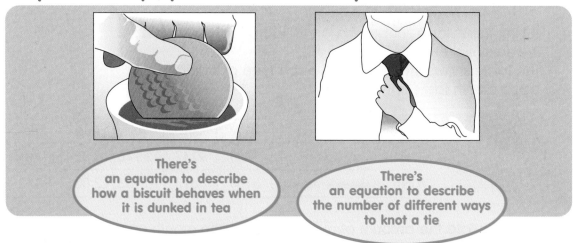

There's an equation to describe how a biscuit behaves when it is dunked in tea

There's an equation to describe the number of different ways to knot a tie

1 Looking Back

1. For each picture, work out what the letter is worth:

a

Total = 26

b

All the weights are in kg.

c

£12

£n is removed from the bag leaving £2

2. For each number machine, work backwards to get the **IN** number:

a IN   OUT   b IN   OUT   c IN   OUT

(k) – 5 (8)   (c) + 2 (8)   (y) × 9 (45)

3. Solve these equations:

    a $n + 3 = 14$ b $k - 7 = 9$ c $7x = 14$

    d $7 + y = 14$ e $7 = h - 3$ f $14 = e + 14$

4. A book costs £x. A pencil case costs £3.
   Write down an expression in x for:

   a the cost of four books
   b the cost of three books and a pencil case
   c the change from £20 when I buy one book.

5. Write down an equation suggested by each picture. All the weights are in kg.

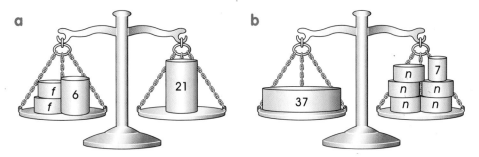

a   b

6. a Iain bought six chocolates.
   Each cost x pence.
   Write an expression in x for their total cost.
   b The shop charges 10 pence for the box.
   Write an expression in x for the cost of six chocolates and a box.
   c The actual cost is 40 pence.
   Make an equation and solve it to find the cost of one chocolate.

2 The Great Equation Cover-up

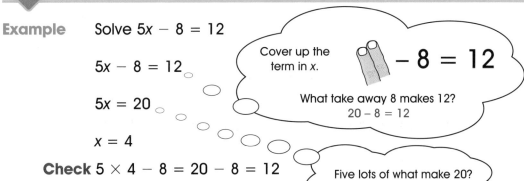

Example Solve $5x - 8 = 12$

$5x - 8 = 12$

$5x = 20$

$x = 4$

Check $5 \times 4 - 8 = 20 - 8 = 12$

Cover up the term in x.

$\boxed{} - 8 = 12$

What take away 8 makes 12?
$20 - 8 = 12$

Five lots of what make 20?
Five lots of 4 makes 20.

A

1. Solve each equation using the cover-up method:

   a $x + 6 = 10$ b $y + 8 = 22$ c $m + 14 = 14$ d $n + 5 = 12$
   e $z - 5 = 10$ f $k - 7 = 1$ g $t - 4 = 19$ h $g - 8 = 7$
   i $p - 6 = 6$ j $7 - z = 1$ k $21 - x = 12$ l $15 - g = 1$

2. Two more people than yesterday turned up for Gym.

   a Let x stand for the number who turned up yesterday.
      Write down an expression in x for the number who turned up today.
   b The actual number who turned up today was 12.
      i   Form an equation in x.
      ii Solve it to find how many turned up yesterday.

3. Solve each equation:

   a $3x = 18$ b $5y = 45$ c $7t = 56$ d $9k = 108$ e $12d = 60$
   f $11p = 121$ g $13q = 52$ h $15g = 60$ i $17m = 85$ j $21z = 105$
   k $\frac{1}{3}r = 12$ l $\frac{1}{2}t = 6$ m $\frac{1}{5}k = 13$ n $\frac{1}{4}n = 16$ o $\frac{1}{7}x = 3$

4. Because she'd been practising, Maria managed to do three times as
    many problems this week as she did last week.

   a Let y stand for the number she did last week.
      Write down an expression in y for the number of problems she
      managed this week.

   b She managed 60 problems this week.
      i   Write down an equation in y.
      ii Solve it to find how many problems she did last week.

5. The car is 4 m long. Three buses and a car form a queue.

   a Let the length of a bus be b metres.
      Form an expression in b for the length of the queue.
   b The queue is 31 m long.
      Form an equation in b to find the length of a bus.

6. Solve each equation by the cover-up method.
    Check your solution is correct.

   a $22 - 3x = 4$ b $18 - 3x = 3$ c $17 - 4x = 9$ d $100 - 5x = 55$
   e $23 - 6x = 5$ f $64 - 4y = 32$ g $39 - 12y = 3$ h $47 - 7z = 12$
   i $17 - 2k = 1$ j $18 - 9y = 0$

7. James started with £86 in the bank.
He took out the same amount each week for four weeks.

   a Let x represent what was taken out each week.
     Write down an expression in x for what is left in James' account.
   b He has £38 left in the bank.
     Form an equation in x and solve it to find how much James
     withdrew each week.

B

1. Solve each equation by the cover-up method:

   a $2y - 5 = 1$ **b** $6 + 3x = 12$ **c** $29 = 5m + 4$ **d** $36 = 8 + 4n$
   e $20 - 2k = 10$ **f** $0 = 27 - 9a$ **g** $21 = 12r - 3$ **h** $4 + 3a = 19$

2. Now solve each of these equations:

   a $18 - \frac{1}{2}k = 14$ **b** $3 = \frac{1}{3}x - 2$ **c** $5 = 8 - \frac{1}{6}y$ **d** $\frac{1}{3}x - 7 = 3$
   e $\frac{1}{2}c - 3 = 2$ **f** $\frac{1}{4}p + 3 = 5$ **g** $10 = \frac{1}{3}y + 7$ **h** $1 = \frac{1}{5}n - 3$

3.

I think of a number. I treble it. I add 9. The result is 30.

   a Let x represent the number I first thought of.
     Form an expression in x for:
     i   the number trebled
     ii the result after 9 is added.

   b Form an equation in x and solve it to find my number.
   c Use the same method for finding my number in the following cases:
     i   I think of a number. I quarter it. I subtract 5. The result is 4.
     ii I think of a number. I double it. I take the answer from 20.
        The result is 12.

4. For each equation simplify the left-hand side before solving the equation:

   a $17 - 2x - 5 = 0$ **b** $23 - 5y - 8 = 5$ **c** $41 - 10x - 11 = 10$
   d $5y - y + 3 = 31$ **e** $12 + 5x - x = 20$ **f** $8 + n + 2 + 3n = 38$
   g $6x + 14 - 2x - 3 = 43$ **h** $x + 1 + x + 2 = 11$ **i** $5y - 4 - 3y - 2 = 0$

3 A Balanced Approach

Imagine an equation is a set of scales that are balanced.
As long as we do the same thing, add, subtract, multiply or divide, to both sides, the results must also balance.

Example   Solve $9x + 17 = 143$

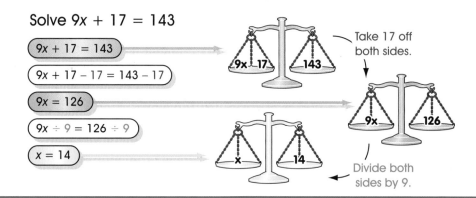

$9x + 17 = 143$

$9x + 17 - 17 = 143 - 17$

$9x = 126$

$9x \div 9 = 126 \div 9$

$x = 14$

Take 17 off both sides.

Divide both sides by 9.

A

1. Solve each equation by keeping the balance, showing each step carefully:

   a $5x + 25 = 90$ b $8y + 27 = 83$ c $6z + 84 = 150$
   d $7x + 99 = 190$ e $12x + 14 = 194$ f $4h + 43 = 79$

2. Seven little ants form a line.
   The ant at the front carries a 9 mm leaf.
   Altogether it forms a 100 mm queue.

   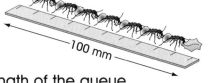

   a Let x mm be the length of one ant.
      Write down an expression in x for the length of the queue.
   b Form an equation in x.
   c What is the length of one ant?

3. Martin looked at the equation $25 - 3x = 10$.

   a He added $3x$ to both sides.
      What is $25 - 3x + \mathbf{3x}$?
   b What does the equation become?
   c Now solve the equation for Martin.

4. Solve the following by a similar method:

   a $75 - 6x = 3$ b $127 - 4y = 67$ c $109 - 5z = 54$
   d $39 - 2x = 23$ e $34 - 4x = 6$ f $88 - 7k = 46$
   g $41 - 17k = 24$ h $73 - 5g = 33$

5. In the cupboard there were 325 jotters. The teacher removed 17 packets.

 a Let x represent the number of jotters in one packet.
  Form an expression in x for the number of jotters now left in the cupboard.
 b There are only 121 jotters left in the cupboard.
  Form an equation in x and solve it to find the number of jotters in a packet.

 4 Inequations

The ant is bigger than the leaf it is carrying.
If the ant is x mm long and the leaf is 9 mm long,
we could write $x > 9$.
The symbol $>$ is read as is bigger than.

In mathematics we use the following symbols:

$x = 4$ x equals 4

$x < 4$ x is smaller than 4   0, 1, 2, 3 are whole number solutions.

$x \le 4$ x is smaller than or equal to 4   0, 1, 2, 3, 4 are whole number solutions.

$x > 4$ x is bigger than 4   Numbers 5 and over are whole number solutions.

$x \ge 4$ x is bigger than or equal to 4   Numbers 4 and over are whole number solutions.

Example   My speed is v mph. I am driving legally.
Write down an inequation in v to describe the situation.

Solution: $v \le 30$

 A

1. Use either $<$ or $>$ between each pair of numbers to make a true statement: a 4   8   b 1   2   c 9   3   d 2   1

2. Choosing solutions from $\{0, 1, 2, 3, 4\}$, solve these inequations:

 a $x < 2$ b $x > 3$ c $x \le 1$ d $x \ge 4$ e $x \le 4$ f $x > 3$

3. Describe each situation using an inequation:

 a My lorry weighs x tonnes and is too heavy to cross the bridge.
 b I am travelling at y miles per hours and not breaking the speed limit.
 c I travel a further m km and have passed through the kangaroo area.

d Remember that the heavier weight will be lower on the scales.

i

ii

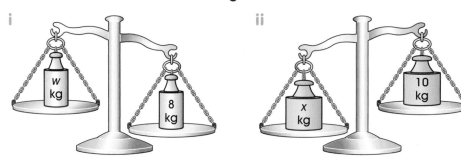

e I have £*n* but cannot afford a ticket.

Tickets Cost £2·50

f There are *w* pupils in the class but there are enough books for one to each pupil.

4. a

b

c

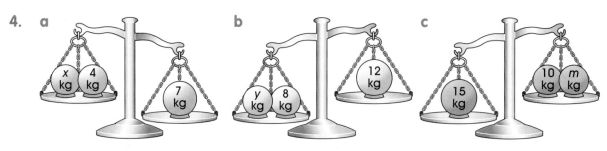

Choose from:
{2 kg, 3 kg, 4 kg, 5 kg}

Choose from:
{3 kg, 4 kg, 5 kg, 6 kg}

Choose from:
{4 kg, 5 kg, 6 kg, 7 kg}

i Describe each picture using an inequation.
ii Give the possible solutions from the listed weights.

5. Solve these inequations, choosing solutions from {3, 4, 5, 6, 7}:

a $x - 1 \geq 4$ **b** $x + 5 \leq 9$ **c** $4 > x - 2$
d $7 < 1 + x$ **e** $10 - x \leq 3$ **f** $11 + x > 18$

B

1. Match each inequation with one of the solutions.
   The solutions were chosen from {0, 1, 2, 3, 4, 5, 6}.

   Inequations
   a $4 + 5x < 14$
   b $2x + 1 > 9$
   c $20 - 3x \leq 2$
   d $20 \leq 5x + 5$
   e $14 < 20 - x$
   f $6 - x \geq 3$

   Solutions
   i $x = 6$
   ii $x = 0, 1, 2, 3, 4$ or 5
   iii $x = 3, 4, 5$ or 6
   iv $x = 5$ or 6
   v $x = 0$ or 1
   vi $x = 0, 1, 2$ or 3

2. Solve these inequations choosing solutions from {1, 2, 3, 4, 5, 6, 7, 8, 9, 10}:

   a $3x - 1 \geq 17$ b $2x - 1 < 5$ c $40 < 4x + 8$
   d $8 \geq 15 - x$ e $11 - x \geq 9$ f $20 - 2x < 10$
   g $3x + 20 \leq 5x + 2$ h $40 - 2x \leq 31 + x$ i $50 - 3x \leq 49 - 2x$

Challenge

The Five Unbalanced Balances

Each weight on these balances weighs a whole number of kilograms.
Use the information from all five balances to determine the value of x
and of y.

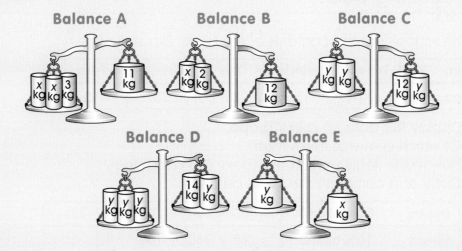

Balance A   Balance B   Balance C

Balance D   Balance E

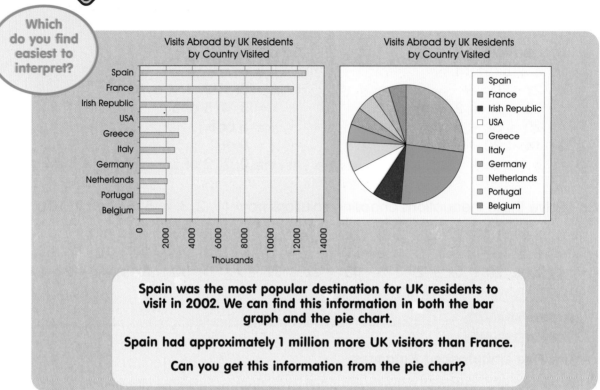

Which do you find easiest to interpret?

Visits Abroad by UK Residents by Country Visited

Thousands

Visits Abroad by UK Residents by Country Visited

- Spain
- France
- Irish Republic
- USA
- Greece
- Italy
- Germany
- Netherlands
- Portugal
- Belgium

Spain was the most popular destination for UK residents to visit in 2002. We can find this information in both the bar graph and the pie chart.

Spain had approximately 1 million more UK visitors than France.

Can you get this information from the pie chart?

1 Looking Back

1. At the school fête the contents of the Lucky Dip stall were:

Item	Erasers	Sweets	Toys	Pencils	Pens
Frequency	20	15	30	25	10

a   Display this data on a bar graph.
b   Of which item was there most?
c   How many items were in the Lucky Dip altogether?
d   Copy and complete the table below:

Erasers	20% of 360°	= (20 × 360) ÷ 100	72°
Sweets	15% of 360°	= (15 × 360) ÷ 100	
Toys	30% of 360°	= (30 × 360) ÷ 100	
Pencils	25% of 360°		
Pens	10% of 360°		

e   Draw a pie chart of the data.
f   Which two items added together made up half of the total Lucky Dip?

2. One of the stalls at the fête was called **Guess the Weight of the Cake**.
   The number of guesses is shown below:

Weight (kg)	0·80	0·85	0·90	0·95	1·00	1·05	1·10	1·15	1·20	1·25	1·30	1·35
Frequency	4	1	14	6	10	16	14	15	11	6	3	1

   a Draw a frequency polygon to display this data.
   b What was the most frequently chosen weight?
   c The cost of one guess was 15p.
      Draw a data table to record the money raised at each of
      the weights above.
   d What was the total money raised on this stall?
   e The cake weighed 872 grams. Why did this make prize-giving easy?

3. The takings from the different stalls at the fête were gathered and counted
   each hour. The takings are shown on the tables below:

 Cake Stall

Hour	Takings
1	£2·10
2	£1·05
3	£2·55
4	£6·75
5	£1·65
6	£1·05

 Lucky Dip

Hour	Takings
1	£2·30
2	£2·70
3	£4·00
4	£5·90
5	£3·00
6	£2·10

 Hoopla

Hour	Takings
1	£3·35
2	£4·10
3	£2·90
4	£6·55
5	£3·35
6	£1·90

 Beat the Goalie

Hour	Takings
1	£4·55
2	£6·25
3	£7·30
4	£7·10
5	£4·55
6	£2·35

Face Painting

Hour	Takings
1	£3·25
2	£4·40
3	£1·95
4	£3·80
5	£2·10
6	£1·30

   a Copy and complete the table to show the overall hourly takings:

Hour	1	2	3	4	5	6
Overall Takings (£)						

   b Draw a line graph to display the data.
   c Describe the trend shown on the graph.
   d Copy and complete the table to show the overall takings from each
      stall:

Stall	Cake	Lucky Dip	Hoopla	Goalie	Face Paint
Overall Takings (£)					

   e Draw a bar graph to display the data.
   f i Which stall made most money?   ii Which stall made least money?

4. Mrs Brown gives away free cups of soup at the fête. She keeps a check on the temperature of the soup as she heats it, recording it each minute.

Time (min)	Temp. (°C)
0	20
1	23
2	29
3	37
4	48
5	65
6	88

a Draw a line graph to display the data, joining the points with a smooth curve.
b The soup is ready to serve at 65°C.
How long should Mrs Brown heat each pot she makes?

2   Interpreting Diagrams and Tables

 A

1. Mrs Kendall's class carried out an investigation into the number of brothers or sisters everyone in the class has.

The data is displayed in the diagram below:

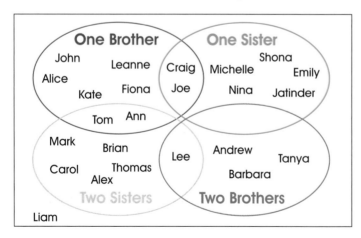

The whole class can be found inside the box.

Those pupils with exactly one brother are inside the red circle.

Those with exactly one sister are inside the green circle.

Those with one brother and one sister will be inside both red and green circles.

a   Are there any pupils with no siblings (brothers or sisters)?
b   Who has the most siblings?
c   i   How many brothers does Nina have?
   ii   How many sisters does Ann have?
   iii   Does Barbara have a sister?
   iv   How many siblings does Craig have?
   v   How many people have two sisters?
   vi   How many people have at least one brother?
d   How many siblings does the class have in total?

2.   A survey in the class of how each pupil liked their tea produced the following:

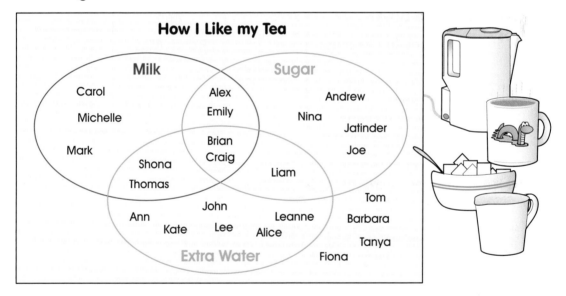

a   i   How many took milk?
   ii   Who took milk only?

b   Who took milk and sugar?
c   Who took sugar and extra water but no milk?
d   How does Tom like his tea?

Diagrams like these are called Venn diagrams **after their inventor, John Venn.**

◆ **Investigate**

Ask your class three questions.

❖ Do you walk to school?
❖ Do you take school lunches?
❖ Are you a boy?

Draw a Venn diagram to illustrate your findings.

3. Mrs Kendall's class decided to investigate the number of
   right- and left-handed boys and girls within the class.
   The data is displayed in the diagram:

   a i How many are
         in the class?
      ii How many are boys?
      iii What fraction of the
         class are boys?

   b i How many in the class
         are girls?
      ii How many girls are
         left-handed?
      iii What fraction of the
         girls are left-handed?

	Girls	Boys
Left-handed	Michelle Leanne Ann	Jatinder Andrew
Right-handed	Fiona Alice Shona Emily Tanya Carol Nina Kate Barbara	Liam Brian Tom John Mark Craig Alex Lee Joe Thomas

   c What fraction of the boys are right-handed?
   d What fraction of the class are left-handed?

Diagrams like these are called Carroll diagrams **after Lewis Carroll, who invented
them. He wrote** Alice in Wonderland**, too.**

◆ **Challenge**

Lewis Carroll also invented puzzles called **word ladders**. Try this one:

Turn FOUR into FIVE.

You have to change one letter at a time, and after each change you
must still have a word. For example, FOUR can change to FOUL.

4. The tables below contain data on all of the middle and upper primary classes.

Primary 4

Male	12	Left-handed	2
		Right-handed	10
Female	14	Left-handed	1
		Right-handed	13

Primary 5

Male	16	Left-handed	1
		Right-handed	15
Female	10	Left-handed	0
		Right-handed	10

Primary 6

Male	17	Left-handed	3
		Right-handed	14
Female	14	Left-handed	2
		Right-handed	12

Primary 7

Male	11	Left-handed	0
		Right-handed	11
Female	19	Left-handed	2
		Right-handed	17

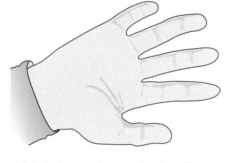

a Which is the largest class?
b Out of all four classes:
 i are there more boys or girls
 ii are most of the girls right-handed or left-handed
 iii are most of the boys right-handed or left-handed
 iv are there more left-handed boys or girls?

c Draw one table to summarise all of the data from the four classes.

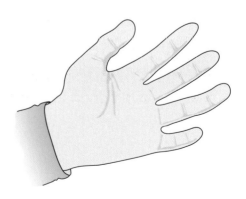

1. As part of a topic on Tourism, three Primary 6 children carried out a holiday survey. Each pupil asked people to complete the survey at various positions around the town.

The table summarises their data:

Researcher		Anita	Gina	Tom
Position		Shops	Library	Pool
Holiday in	United Kingdom	17	33	15
	Abroad	26	16	21
Stayed at	Hotel	7	18	13
	Bed & Breakfast	16	20	9
	Camping	10	9	8
	Other	10	2	6
Length of stay	Less than 7 days	15	14	11
	7–13 day	21	21	20
	Two weeks or more	7	14	5
Weather	Fine	17	10	18
	Fair	16	16	9
	Poor	4	8	3
	Varied	6	15	6

a How many people were surveyed by:
   i Anita   ii Gina   iii Tom?

b How many people were surveyed altogether?

c What was the most common:
   i length of stay
   ii accommodation?

d Did more people camp or stay in bed & breakfast?

e Did more people holiday abroad or in the United Kingdom?

f Draw a pie chart to display the weather data collected by Tom.

3 Interpreting Graphs

A

1. The heights of three plants are monitored for three weeks. The graph shows the results:

   a What would be a suitable title for this graph?

   b Were all of the seedlings the same size when the first height measurement was taken?

   c Which plant had the smallest change in height over the three weeks?

   d What was the difference in heights between plants 1 and 3 at week 2 of the experiment?

   e Which graph's trend is best described by 'The plant grew steadily week by week.'?

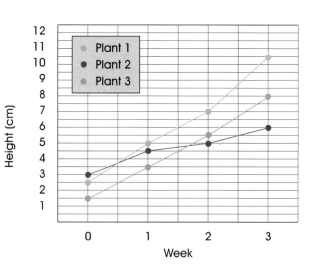

2. The eye colours of pupils in two classes are shown below:

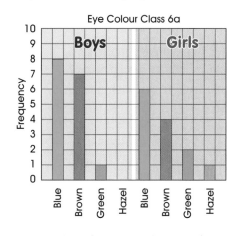

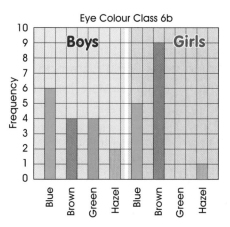

   a How many pupils are there in: i Class 6a   ii Class 6b?
   b Which is the most common eye colour in: i Class 6a   ii Class 6b?
   c Which is the most common eye colour among the boys in both classes?
   d Which is the most common eye colour among the girls in both classes?
   e How many more boys than girls have green eyes?
   f Among both classes, how many more children have brown eyes than hazel eyes?

3. Burnblea Junior Athletics Club have special training shoes designed showing their club logo. They decide to investigate the most frequent shoe sizes among their members. Each coach is asked to collect the data and display it on a graph.

   a Name the different types of graph shown.
   b How many of the athletes wear a:
      i size 2 shoe   ii size 13 shoe   iii size 5 shoe?

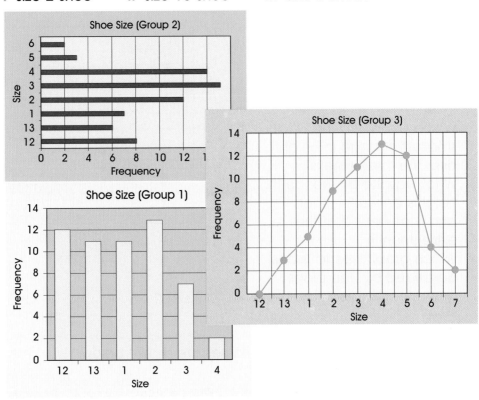

   c What is the most frequent shoe size of all three groups?
   d Which is the least common shoe size of all three groups?
   e Which group do you think represents the youngest athletes?

4. The lines on this graph represent multiplication tables. The blue line represents the two times table.

   a Which multiplication table is shown by the:
      i red line on the graph
      ii yellow line on the graph?

   b Copy and extend the graph to display the multiplication tables of 5, 6, 7, 8, 9.

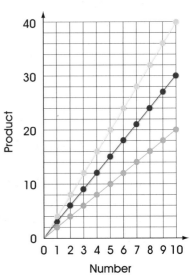

4 Interpreting Pie Charts

A

1. The pie charts below contain data on numbers of animal species legally protected in Scotland since 1954:

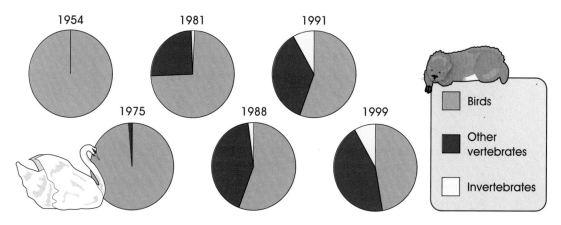

1954   1981   1991

1975   1988   1999

Birds

Other vertebrates

Invertebrates

a In 1954, were there any:
   i   invertebrate animals protected
   ii birds protected
   iii vertebrates, other than birds, protected?

b When did the first:
   i   vertebrates, other than birds, become protected
   ii invertebrates become protected?

c Which group (birds, other vertebrates or invertebrates) has always made up the smallest number of protected species in Scotland?

d Give the approximate percentage of bird species protected compared to the overall protected species in 1981.

e Which group (birds, other vertebrates or invertebrates) has had more protected species than the other groups at every recording?

f Can we tell from the pie charts if the number of birds species is more now than it was in 1954? Explain your answer.

2. The chart shows the data collected while observing a bird table. The type of bird to visit is noted for 240 visits.

a What type of bird visits the table most commonly?

b How many: i sparrows   ii robins
   visited the table?

c How many more starlings than blackbirds visited?

Visits to the Bird Table

☐ Sparrow
☐ Starling
☐ Robin
☐ Blackbird

240 visits

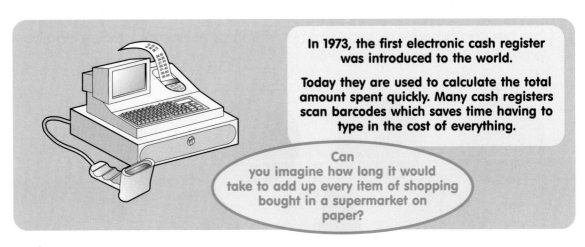

Unit 18 > Decimals

In 1973, the first electronic cash register was introduced to the world.

Today they are used to calculate the total amount spent quickly. Many cash registers scan barcodes which saves time having to type in the cost of everything.

Can you imagine how long it would take to add up every item of shopping bought in a supermarket on paper?

1 > Looking Back

1. Work out these additions and subtractions:

   a $86 \cdot 7 + 18 \cdot 25$ b $223 \cdot 9 + 36 \cdot 28$ c $46 \cdot 3 - 18 \cdot 18$ d $80 - 37 \cdot 25$
   e $447 \cdot 8 + 9 \cdot 73$ f $101 \quad 57 \cdot 22$ g $65 \cdot 67 + 48 \cdot 8$ h $326 - 7 \cdot 77$
   i $808 \cdot 4 + 79 \cdot 66$ j $500 - 77 \cdot 4$

2. Calculate mentally:

   a $8 \cdot 6 + 6 \cdot 3$ b $14 \cdot 3 + 8 \cdot 6$ c $13 \cdot 6 - 4 \cdot 5$ d $19 \cdot 9 - 7 \cdot 7$ e $18 \cdot 2 + 9 \cdot 5$
   f $20 \cdot 7 - 3 \cdot 4$ g $12 \cdot 5 + 11 \cdot 4$ h $30 \cdot 2 - 5 \cdot 1$ i $33 \cdot 6 - 11 \cdot 2$ j $16 \cdot 5 + 3 \cdot 6$

3. The total weight of your luggage, when travelling on an Air Scotia flight, must be less than 22 kg.

   a Colin's suitcase was $8 \cdot 78$ kg under the limit.
      What was the weight of his suitcase?
   b Jane had two bags weighing $11 \cdot 7$ kg and $9 \cdot 38$ kg.
      How much under the baggage limit was she?

4. Sarita bought a new DVD for £14·89 and a Game Station game for £33·75. She paid with three £20 notes. What was her change?

5. Round each of these numbers to 1 decimal place.

   a $8 \cdot 27$ b $33 \cdot 24$ c $1 \cdot 278$ d $0 \cdot 467$ e $87 \cdot 29$

6. Estimate the answer to each calculation by first rounding the parts to 1 decimal place:

   a 3·126 + 4·778   b 18·22 + 8·59   c 22·954 − 7·212
   d 30·81 − 9·62   e 24·334 + 7·721 f 40·121 − 9·951

7. A scientist keeps special liquids in large glass beakers.

   A   B   C   D

   1·315   1·079   0·961   0·855
   litres   litres   litres   litres

   a Round each volume to 1 decimal place.
   b Which two beakers have a volume of about 2 litres?

8. Calculate:

   a 42·7 × 4   b 27·65 × 7   c 110·7 ÷ 3   d 134·3 × 6   e 84·36 ÷ 6
   f 127·7 × 6   g 49·2 ÷ 5   h 99·78 × 9   i 391·4 ÷ 4   j 436 ÷ 8

9. A decorator needed eight 12·75 litre tins of emulsion to finish a painting job. How many litres did he use in total?

10. Mr and Mrs Doby bought a set of six stone plant urns at their local garden centre.
    The total weight of all the urns is 91·5 kg.
    What is the weight of one plant urn?

11. The McIntyre family hired a car to tour different parts of Scotland on holiday.
    If the cost of car hire was £21·89 per day:

    a How much did they pay for 5 days hire?
    b They drove a total distance of 491·1 km during their time away.
       How far, on average, did they travel each day?

12. a Simon got a new digital camera and paid for it in six equal monthly installments. Each monthly payment is £ 23·76.
       How much did the camera cost?
    b Micha spotted a music system she liked which was reduced to £214. She paid for it over eight months. Work out the cost of each monthly payment.

5. **a** Mrs Rashid bought a new car from Mega Motors.
        She saved £1837·50 by taking advantage of an offer.
        The usual cost of the car is £10 499·99. How much did Mrs Rashid pay?
    b Mr Spencer paid £10 642·08 for his new car.
        He made a massive saving of £2257·41.
        What was the original price of the car?

Challenge

a Nasim and his mum drove 36·311 km from Cairnmore to Fencedyke.
    What route did they take?
b Is this the shortest route?
Explain your answer.

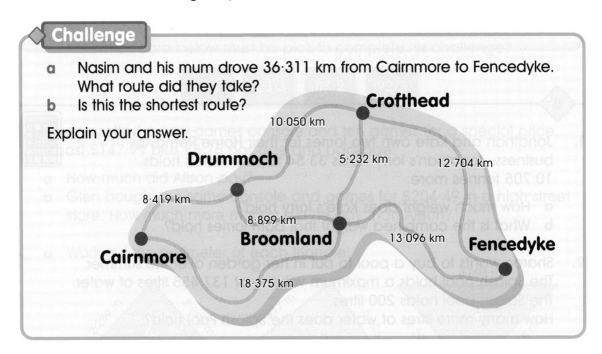

Investigate

Sort these cards into two equal piles so that the total of each pile is 50.

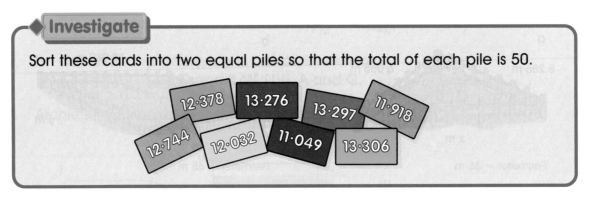

4   # Multiplying and Dividing with a Calculator

A

1. A bottle of Foamy bubble bath has a volume of 0·25 litres.
    Work out the total volume there would be in:

    a 24   **b** 85   **c** 160   **d** 200 bottles.

2. What number comes out of each function machine?

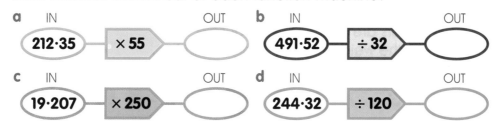

a IN   OUT   b IN   OUT

212·35   × 55   491·52   ÷ 32

c IN   OUT   d IN   OUT

19·207   × 250   244·32   ÷ 120

3. Linda ordered a new sofa from the catalogue for £475·20.
   She was given the choice of spreading the cost over 24 weeks, 60 weeks
   or 144 weeks. Calculate the weekly payment for:

   a   24 weeks   b   60 weeks   c   144 weeks.

4. During his 14-day cycling holiday, Ryan travelled 337·75 km.
   Calculate the average distance he cycled each day, correct to
   1 decimal place.

5. 1837·5 kg of potatoes are put into 300 bags of the same weight.
   What is the weight of each bag?

6. Bertie's Bakery sells packs of delicious biscuits and cakes.

Cookies
Pack of 8

Doughnuts
Pack of 6

Mini Muffins
Pack of 12

In a week, the shop made:
£130·56 from the sale of 96 packs of cookies
£185·76 from the sale of 129 packs of doughnuts
£403·20 from the sale of 240 packs of mini muffins.

Work out the cost of:
a   one cookie
b   one doughnut
c   one muffin.

Challenge

Nicola keyed a number into her calculator:
Then she divided it by 75.
Next she multiplied the result by 180.
Then she divided this answer by 150.
Finally she multiplied by 48 and got the answer 872·64.

What number did she key in to start with?

A

1. Trace each pair of shapes, then find the size and the centre of the rotation.

a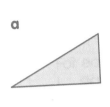

b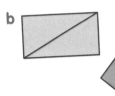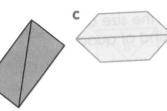

c

2. Use tracing paper to make your own shape and its image after rotation. Give it to a friend to see if they can find the centre and size of the rotation.

◆ **Investigate**

Look through magazines for pictures of rotation and symmetry.
Find the centre and size of the rotation.
Make a poster to illustrate rotation and turn symmetry.

4 ▶ **Tiles**

A shape that can be used to cover a flat surface in a regular fashion without leaving spaces or overlapping is said to **tile**.
An artist called M. C. Escher studied such shapes in great detail. Do an Internet search to find what you can about his work.

In this tiling, the shapes have been both **translated** (moved along) and **reflected** (flipped over).

A

1. This tile is based on one of Escher's tiles.
   Make seven copies by tracing or photocopying and see if you can make them tile using translation and rotation.
   Colour it in to highlight the pattern.
   Hint It's best to use three colours.

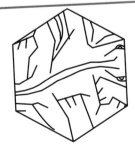

2. This hexagon will tile as shown.
   It has two axes and a centre of
   symmetry.

   a If $a° = 90°$,
      calculate the size of $b°$.
   b If instead $a° = 100°$,
      calculate the size of $b°$.
   c If $b° = 140°$,
      calculate the size of $a°$.

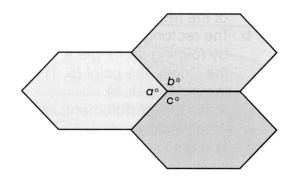

3. a This tiling is based on a kite shape.
      It needs translation (slide four squares to
      the right) and rotation.

      Copy the tiling until one tile is completely
      surrounded.

   b The v-kite will also tile.
      Copy and continue the tiling until one
      shape is completely surrounded.

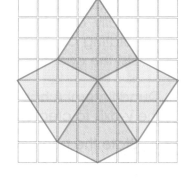

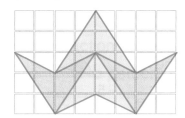

4. A triangular tile has vertices
   A(-5, 4), (-4, 2), (-1, 4).

   It is moved four squares to the right
   (a translation) creating a second tile
   as shown. A has moved to (-1, 4).

   a To what points have the other
      vertices moved?
   b Both tiles are now moved one
      square to the right and two
      squares down. A is now at (-4, 2).

      Draw all four tiles on a grid.

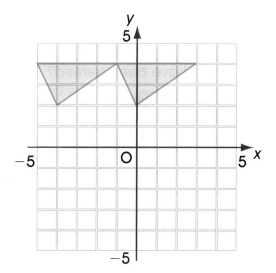

5. In a 4 kg bag of potatoes, $\frac{3}{5}$ had red skins, $\frac{7}{25}$ were big enough for baked potatoes, $\frac{1}{20}$ had shoots coming out of them and the rest were bad.

    a   Express each amount in grams.
    b   What was the weight of the bad potatoes?

Some common fractions and their percentage forms should be known by heart:

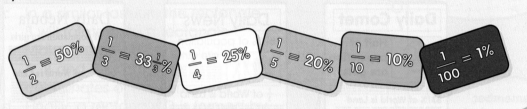

$\frac{1}{2} = 50\%$ $\frac{1}{3} = 33\frac{1}{3}\%$ $\frac{1}{4} = 25\%$ $\frac{1}{5} = 20\%$ $\frac{1}{10} = 10\%$ $\frac{1}{100} = 1\%$

6. Use these facts to help you mentally calculate:

    a   50% of £350   b   25% of £240   c   10% of £340
    d   20% of £550   e   1% of £600   f   33$\frac{1}{3}$% of £60
    g   100% of £430   h   33$\frac{1}{3}$% of £39

Some percentages can be found from others:

75% = 50% + 25%   **30% = 3 × 10%**
5% = $\frac{1}{2}$ of 10%   **60% = 50% + 10%**

7. Use facts like these to help you work out the following mentally:

    a   75% of £8   b   30% of £400   c   5% of £220   d   60% of £70
    e   2% of £500   f   66$\frac{2}{3}$% of £90   g   5% of £80   h   15% of £80

8. In a recent survey about healthy diet, 400 children were asked about their favourite vegetables. 20% liked cauliflower, 33% liked potatoes, 40% liked peas and the rest didn't like vegetables.

    How many liked each kind of vegetable?

9. From each group of three fractions, pick out the largest:

    a $\frac{1}{2}$, 0·45, 55%   b $\frac{2}{3}$, 0·66, 70%   c $\frac{3}{10}$, 0·27, 33%
    d $\frac{2}{5}$, 0·42, 41%   e $\frac{2}{25}$, 0·1, 15%   f $\frac{3}{100}$, 0·7, 5%
    g $\frac{7}{20}$, 0·3, 30%   h $\frac{11}{50}$, 0·2, 21%   i $\frac{2}{2}$, 0·95, 99%

2 Why Decimalise?

Before 1971, the people of Britain had to work with $\frac{1}{12}$, $\frac{1}{20}$, $\frac{1}{240}$
and other fractions when working with money.
They used $\frac{1}{12}$, $\frac{1}{3}$, $\frac{1}{1760}$ and other fractions when working
with length.

In 1971 Britain went **decimal**.
This was because it was easier. Now, we work with $\frac{1}{10}$, $\frac{1}{100}$, $\frac{1}{1000}$ for most things.

A

1. Express the following fractions as: i decimals ii hundredths:

   a $\frac{20}{40}$ b $\frac{16}{32}$ c $\frac{6}{30}$ d $\frac{24}{30}$ e $\frac{24}{32}$ f $\frac{40}{60}$ g $\frac{75}{125}$

2. Express each measurement:
   i as a decimal fraction of a metre   ii in centimetres:

   a $\frac{1}{2}$ m   b $\frac{1}{4}$ m   c $\frac{3}{10}$ m   d $\frac{4}{5}$ m   e $\frac{11}{20}$ m   f $\frac{7}{25}$ m

3. At Christmas, a school used $\frac{4}{5}$ of a 7 m roll of paper for a frieze about
   Christmas trees.

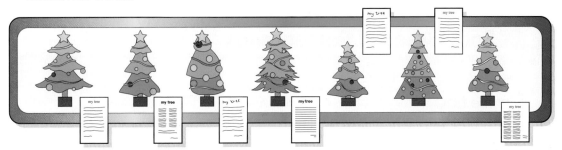

   a How many centimetres did they use?
   b Express this answer as a decimal fraction of a metre.
   c The school also used up $\frac{11}{25}$ of its stock of 75 rolls of crêpe paper.
     How many rolls of crêpe paper did they use?

4. a $\frac{1}{4}$ km   b $\frac{4}{5}$ km   c $\frac{7}{10}$ km   d $\frac{13}{20}$ km
   e $\frac{3}{25}$ km   f $\frac{7}{100}$ km   g $\frac{135}{1000}$ km   h $\frac{3}{1000}$ km

   Write each distance:
   i as a decimal fraction of a kilometre   ii in metres.

5. Calculate the following amounts, giving your answers in pounds:

   a $\frac{2}{3}$ of £333   b $\frac{3}{4}$ of £564   c $\frac{4}{5}$ of £455   d $\frac{3}{10}$ of £2300

B

1. Susan lived 2·3 km from the school.
Each morning her mum gave her a lift
$\frac{9}{10}$ of the way.

   a How far did her lift take her?
   b How far did she still have to walk?

Express each of the answers in kilometres.

2. A school raised £2800 from sales of tickets for their concert.
They had to pay $\frac{1}{4}$ of the money to the publishers of the play.
They used $\frac{2}{5}$ of the money for costumes and props.
$\frac{1}{20}$ paid for the production of tickets, programmes and posters.
$\frac{3}{10}$ was used to give the children a treat at the end.

   a How much money from the concert was spent on each item of
expenditure?
   b The firm that produced the programmes, tickets and posters gave $\frac{2}{7}$ of
the money they received from the school to a children's charity.
How much money did they give to the charity?
   c The principal actor in the play was so good his parents gave him £25 to
spend. He spent $\frac{1}{4}$ of it on presents for his family, $\frac{3}{8}$ on magazines and
the rest on sweets. How much did he spend on each item?

 3 **Some Uses of Percentages**

The label shows the make-up
of the hat.
What percentage is nylon?

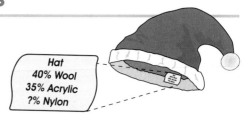

$100\% - 40\% - 35\% = 25\%$

A

1. Find the missing percentage for each of these labels:

b

a

c

2. At a school sale of work, there was a rich fruit cake for sale.
    It weighed 1·5 kg.

    50% of the weight was sultanas and raisins.
    20% was flour.
    25% was sugar.
    The rest was milk and eggs.

    a   Calculate the weight of each ingredient in the cake.
    b   What percentage was milk and eggs?

3. A fair raised £460 for school funds.
    The book stall made 25% of the total, the cake and candy stall 30%,
    the raffle 40% and the rest was a donation from a friend of the school.

    a   Calculate how much was raised by each stall.
    b   What percentage was raised by donation?
    c   How much money was the donation?

4. A biscuit manufacturer ran a special offer.
    Every packet of biscuits was increased in
    weight by 12%.

    What is the new weight of each of the
    following packets:

    a   Digestive biscuits 500 g   b   Ginger snaps 200 g
    c   Chocolate biscuits 600 g   d   Chocolate chip cookies 300 g
    e   Small tin of assorted biscuits 1 kg

5.

    Work out the new amounts in each bottle:

    a   Shower gel 220 ml   b   Family size shampoo $\frac{1}{2}$ litre
    c   Hand-wash soap dispenser 400 ml   d   Cleansing lotion 120 ml
    e   Deodorant 180 ml

4 **Mental Practice**

Examples

Find 40% of 300
40% = 4 × 10%
= 4 × 30
= 120

Find 5% of 60
5% = $\frac{1}{2}$ of 10%
= $\frac{1}{2}$ of 6
= 3

Find 2$\frac{1}{2}$% of 60
2$\frac{1}{2}$% = $\frac{1}{2}$ of 5%
= $\frac{1}{2}$ of 3
= 1·5

A

1. Calculate the following in a similar way to the above examples:

   a 60% of 200   b 40% of 60   c 30% of 70   d 20% of 650
   e 5% of 40   f 5% of 800   g 2$\frac{1}{2}$% of 800   h 2$\frac{1}{2}$% of 2000

2. Find these percentages mentally. **Hints** are given in brackets.

   a 20% of £2550 [2 × 10%]
   b 25% of $345 [$\frac{1}{2}$ of 50%]
   c 75% of 480 g [3 × 25%]
   d 15% of 12 m [10% + 5%]
   e 40% of £600 [4 × 10%]

   f 60% of 1200 ml [6 × 10%]
   g 80% of 250 cm [8 × 10%]
   h 55% of £2300 [50% + ($\frac{1}{10}$ of 50%)]
   i 35% of $459 [30% + 5%]
   j 31% of 600 m [30% + 1%]

3. Work through these methods step by step to find the answers:

   a 45% of £60

   50% of £60   =
   5% is $\frac{1}{2}$ of 10%   =
   45% is 50% − 5%   =

   b 17$\frac{1}{2}$% of £60
   10% of 60   =
   5% is $\frac{1}{2}$ of 10%   =
   2$\frac{1}{2}$% is $\frac{1}{2}$ of 5%   =
   17$\frac{1}{2}$% = 10% + 5% + 2$\frac{1}{2}$%   =

4. Use the method suggested above to help you calculate these amounts:

   a 15% of £30   b 15% of £25   c 15% of £36   d 15% of £72
   e 15% of £150   f 12% of £120   g 11% of £440   h 13% of £12
   i 14% of £15   j 16% of £80   k 17$\frac{1}{2}$% of £60   l 17$\frac{1}{2}$% of £120
   m 17$\frac{1}{2}$% of £240 n 17$\frac{1}{2}$% of £44   o 17$\frac{1}{2}$% of £480 p 4% of £50

B

1. Electricity bills have a 5% tax added to them.

   a Copy and complete the bills for the six families shown.

High Voltage Power Ltd

Electricity Bill

Mr & Mrs Smith   A/C No. 01
1 Station Road
Poppleburn

Electricity charge	£ 320
Tax at 5%	£
Total Due	£

High Voltage Power Ltd

Electricity Bill

Mr & Mrs Green   A/C No. 11
2 Station Road
Poppleburn

Electricity charge	£ 460
Tax at 5%	£
Total Due	£

High Voltage Power Ltd

Electricity Bill

Mr & Mrs Edwards   A/C No. 514
3 Station Road
Poppleburn

Electricity charge	£ 280
Tax at 5%	£
Total Due	£

High Voltage Power Ltd

Electricity Bill

Mr & Mrs Jones   A/C No. 349
4 Station Road
Poppleburn

Electricity charge	£ 620
Tax at 5%	£
Total Due	£

High Voltage Power Ltd

Electricity Bill

Mr & Mrs Rashid   A/C No. 180
5 Station Road
Poppleburn

Electricity charge	£ 330
Tax at 5%	£
Total Due	£

High Voltage Power Ltd

Electricity Bill

Mr & Mrs Adams   A/C No. 129
6 Station Road
Poppleburn

Electricity charge	£ 390
Tax at 5%	£
Total Due	£

   b Five of the families have their roofs insulated.
     Which family do you think did not have its roof insulated?
     Give a reason for your answer.

2. In an attempt to save for a holiday, Mr & Mrs McGregor cut back on their expenditures by $17\frac{1}{2}\%$. Below are their expenses for last month. Calculate how much they hope to save on each item of expenditure next month.

   a Electricity bill £260   b Food bill £160   c Clothes £80
   d Telephone £90   e Nights out £70

3. Mark bought all his toiletries in a bargain shop that had reduced all its prices by $7\frac{1}{2}\%$. **Hint** $7\frac{1}{2}\% = 10\% - 2\frac{1}{2}\%$
   Calculate how much he saved on the following items.
   All prices are before reduction.

   a Toothpaste £1·20   b Deodorant £2·40   c Shaving cream £4·80
   d Shampoo £2   e Shower gel £1·60

4. Perfect Fit sold 400 pairs of shoes in one day.
45% of the pairs of shoes sold were black,
35% were blue, 5% were white and 15% were
brown. How many pairs of each colour of shoe did
they sell?

5 Calculator Use

Examples

$\frac{2}{5}$ of 250   40% of 60 $12\frac{1}{2}$% of 240
$2 \div 5 \times 250 = 100$ $40 \div 100 \times 60 = 24$ $12 \cdot 5 \div 100 \times 240 = 30$

A

1. Use a calculator to help you work out the following:

   a $\frac{2}{3}$ of £984   b $\frac{7}{8}$ of £5648   c $\frac{7}{12}$ of 456 km   d $\frac{11}{30}$ of 3600
   e $\frac{4}{5}$ of £3455   f $\frac{3}{4}$ of £6664   g $\frac{7}{100}$ of £480   h $\frac{3}{5}$ of £234

2. Calculate the following amounts:

   a 40% of £4580   b 60% of £2860   c 25% of 6800   d 33% of £3036
   e $12\frac{1}{2}$% of £640   f 7% of £4260   g 9% of £2115   h 24% of £4·50

3. The machines in a knitwear factory were not operating correctly.
   Of the 8748 garments produced, $\frac{2}{3}$ had the wrong design on them and
   another $\frac{1}{12}$ were too small.

   a Calculate how many:
      i had the wrong design   ii were too small.
   b The garments cost £82. The spoilt garments were sold at 45% of the
      original price. How much would these garments be sold for?

4. A school spent £6700 on materials.
   20% of this was spent on paper and pencils, 25% on text books, 18% on
   computer materials,14% on photocopying, 9% on games, 8% on art
   materials and the rest on library books.

   Calculate how much was spent on each category.

Common Sense

In a survey of 130 children, it was reported that 22% ate
an apple after a meal. Using the calculator you find:
22 ÷ 100 × 130 = 28·6 children.

You can't get a fraction of a child so you have to round the answer up to
get an estimate of how many children ate an apple after a meal.

B

1. A school has 180 pupils.
   A week was to be taken off the summer holidays and added to a holiday
   at another time. The pupils were asked when they would prefer to have the
   week's holiday:
   15% wanted to add it to the Christmas holidays.
   23% said the Easter holidays.
   34% said the October break.
   12% said add it to the February break.
   16% wanted a week at the end of May.

   a How many children voted for each suggestion?
   b What do you think the school decided to do? Explain your answer.

2. During a healthy eating week at school, children were asked to watch their
   sugar intake. Calculate, to the nearest gram, how much sugar is in each
   type of biscuit:

   a Jam Cookies 250 g   23% sugar
   b Oat Crunch 266 g   4% sugar
   c Ginger Tea Biscuit 340 g   19% sugar
   d White Chocolate Delight 420 g   29% sugar

3.

The Furniture Store

Great deal at only
8·5% extra
Buy Now!
Pay later!

Calculate how much extra the customers would have to pay when buying:

   a an oak table priced £650   b a rocking chair priced £234
   c a storage chest priced £48   d a computer table priced £120

Unit 21 Two Dimensions

Shapes can be grouped into families, or classes, by looking at their common properties. These shapes have been classified by the number of sides.

Triangles

Quadrilaterals

Pentagons

Hexagons

1 Looking Back

1. Polly made a patchwork quilt.
   What kind of shape is the patch that is:

   a red   b yellow   c green
   d lilac   e blue   f brown?

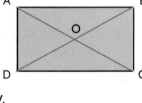

2. ABCD is a rectangle with diagonals that intersect at O:

   a Name a side equal to AB.
   b Name three angles equal to ∠DAC.
   c Name a length equal to AC.
   d Name three lengths equal to OB.
   e What size is ∠DAB?
   f Sketch ABCD and draw in its **two** axes of symmetry.

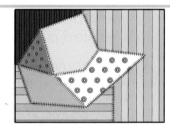

3. PQRS is a square with diagonals that intersect at T:

   a Name three sides equal to PQ.
   b Name seven angles equal to ∠SPR.
   c Name a length equal to PR.
   d Opposite sides of the rectangle and square are parallel.
      What does **parallel** mean?
   e What size is: i ∠SPQ   ii ∠STP?
   f Sketch PQRS and draw in its **four** axes of symmetry.

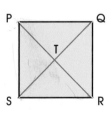

4. a   Use a circular object to draw a circle in your jotter.
    b   Find and mark the centre of the circle.
    c   Draw and label: i a diameter   ii a radius of the circle.
    d   Write down the connection between the radius and diameter of a
        circle.

2 ▶ Quadrilaterals: Nothing Special?

A

1. a   Cut out a set of nine **congruent**
        (identical) quadrilaterals.
        Use two colours if possible, for example
        four red and five blue.
        Label the angles as shown.
    b   Turn the red set through 180°.
    c   Glue a blue one in the centre
        of your jotter.
    d   Surround it by red ones.
    e   Fill the gaps with blue ones.
    f   Notice that the four angles of the
        quadrilateral fit snuggly round each point in the tiling.

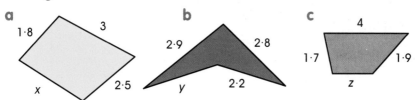

    What is the sum of the four angles of a quadrilateral?

2. a   Calculate the size of the missing angle in each of the following
        quadrilaterals:

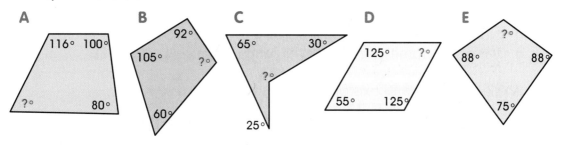

A   116° 100°   ?°   80°

B   92°   105°   ?°   60°

C   65°   30°   ?°   25°

D   125°   ?°   55°   125°

E   ?°   88°   88°   75°

    b   Do any of the above quadrilaterals have:
        i an axis of symmetry   ii a centre of symmetry?

3. Each of the following has a perimeter of 10 cm. Find the length of the
    missing side:

    a   1·8   3   x   2·5

    b   2·9   2·8   y   2·2

    c   4   1·7   1·9   z

3 Special: No Symmetry or One Axis

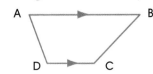

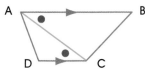

ABCD has a pair of parallel lines.
It is called a **trapezium**.
If we draw a diagonal we form
alternate angles.
Remember Alternate angles are equal.

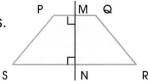

PQRS has a **single axis of symmetry** cutting a pair of sides.
Since it cuts both PQ and SR at right angles, they must be
running in the same direction: they are parallel.
So PQRS is a **symmetrical trapezium**.

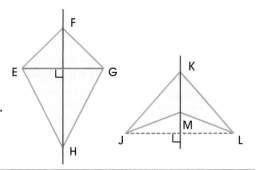

Both EFGH and JKLM have a **single axis of
symmetry** running along a diagonal.
The diagonals cross at right angles.
EFGH and JKLM are called **kites**.
JKLM contains a reflex angle and is a **v-kite**.

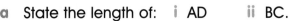

1. ABCD is a kite. Its axis runs along BD.
   AB = 3 cm and DC = 4 cm.

   a State the length of: i AD   ii BC.
   b Calculate the perimeter of the kite.
   c State the size of ∠AEB.
   d Name an angle equal to: i ∠BAE   ii ∠ECD   iii ∠BCD.
   e If it exists, name a line equal in length to: i AB   ii BE   iii EC.

2. WXYZ is a v-kite with axis of symmetry running along XZ.
   WZ = 8 mm and XY = 17 mm.

   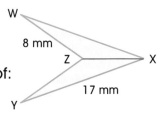

   a State the length of: i WX   ii YZ.
   b Calculate the perimeter of the shape.
   c ∠ZWX = 25° and ∠ZXY = 19°. Calculate the size of:
      i   ∠YXZ   ii   ∠WXY
      iii ∠ZYX   iv the reflex angle ∠WZY.

   d Name the diagonals of the v-kite.

3. Calculate the size of each
   unmarked angle in each
   trapezium. **Hint** What is the
   sum of the angles in a triangle?

   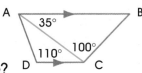

   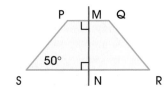

4 Special: Two Axes

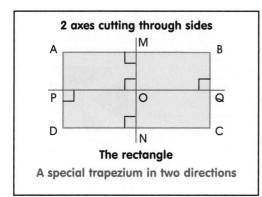

2 axes cutting through sides

The rectangle
A special trapezium in two directions

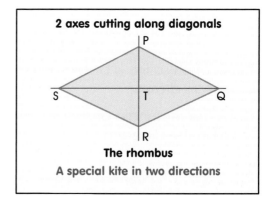

2 axes cutting along diagonals

The rhombus
A special kite in two directions

A

1. Using the rectangle diagram above:

   a Name a length equal to: i AB   ii AD   iii AC.
   b i By thinking of the axis MN, name a length equal to AM.
     ii By thinking of the axis PQ, name another two lengths equal to AM.

   c Name seven lengths equal to AO.

   d i By thinking of the axis MN, name an angle equal to ∠DAB.
     ii By thinking of the axis PQ, name another two angles equal to ∠DAB.

   e Knowing that the four angles of any quadrilateral add up to 360°, calculate the size of each angle in the rectangle.

2. Using the rhombus diagram above:

   a Name a length equal to: i ST   ii PT.
   b Name an angle equal to: i ∠PSR   ii ∠SRQ.

   c i By thinking of the axis PR, name a length equal to SP.
     ii By thinking of the axis SQ, name another two lengths equal to SP.

   d i By thinking of the axis PR, name an angle equal to ∠STP.
     ii By thinking of the axis SQ, name another two angles equal to ∠STP.

   e These four angles add up to 360°.
     i How do we know?
     ii What is the size of each?

   f Copy and complete the following sentences:

   The four sides of a rhombus are ——— .
   Opposite angles of a rhombus are ——— .
   The diagonals of a rhombus cut each other in ——— .[a fraction]
   The diagonals of a rhombus cut each other at ——— .[an angle]

3. What is the length of the side of a rhombus with a perimeter of:

   a 24 cm   b 3·6 m   c 10 mm?

4. If one angle of a rhombus is 30°, what are the sizes of the others?

5. The Scottish saltire is based on a rectangle with its diagonals drawn.

   Copy the rectangle and calculate the size of each angle in the diagram.

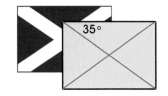

Extra Special: Four Axes

The square has the symmetries of the rectangle **and** the symmetries of the rhombus, so the square has the properties of both.

We can think of the square as a special rectangle or as a special rhombus when solving problems.

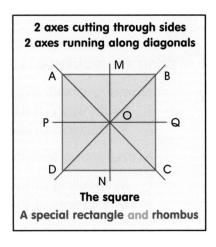

2 axes cutting through sides
2 axes running along diagonals

The square
A special rectangle and rhombus

1. In the square above, AM = 4 cm.

   a Calculate:
      i   the length of AB   ii   the length of BQ
      iii the length of PQ   iv   the perimeter of ABCD.

   b To 1 decimal place, AO = 5·7 cm.
      Calculate the size of:
      i AC   ii BD   iii OC.

   c A fly went a walk from P to O to A to B to D.
      How far did it walk?

   d Make a sketch of the diagram and enter the sizes of as many angles as you can.

2. The green arrowhead of a traffic sign is based on four squares tiling as shown. The side of one square is 3 m and its diagonal is 4·2 m to 1 decimal place.

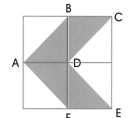

   a Calculate the size of:
      i ∠BAF   ii ∠AFE   iii reflex ∠CDE.

   b What is the sum of the angles in the green hexagon?

   c Calculate the perimeter of the green hexagon to 1 decimal place.

3. At what angle do the diagonals of a square intersect?

4. Calculate the side of a square whose perimeter is:

   a 48 mm   b 36 m   c 1 m.

6 ◆ Special: A Centre of Symmetry

A quadrilateral with half-turn symmetry is called a **parallelogram**.

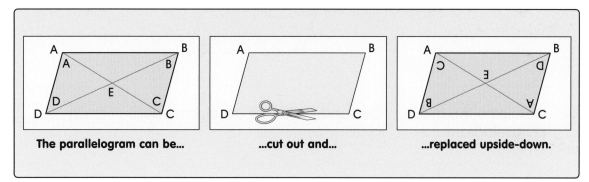

| The parallelogram can be... | ...cut out and... | ...replaced upside-down. |

A

1. In the diagram above, when the shape is turned upside down, A goes to C and D goes to B.

   a Where does: i B go   ii C go?

   b Since A goes to C and D goes to B, then the line AD goes to CB. Where does the line AB go?

   c If AD fits along CB, then AD = CB. Name a line equal to: i AB   ii AE   iii EB.

   d Is there a line equal to AC?

   e i   Where does ∠DAB end up?
      ii Name an angle equal to ∠DAB.

f Name an angle equal to ∠ADC.

g i Name an angle equal to ∠ADB.

   ii Note that ∠ADB and ∠DBC are alternate angles.
     What does this tell us about AD and BC?

h How can we tell that AB is parallel to DC?

i Copy and complete:

Opposite sides of a parallelogram are ——— . [to do with size]

Opposite sides of a parallelogram are ——— . [to do with direction]

Opposite angles of a parallelogram are ——— .

The diagonals of a parallelogram don't have to be ——— .

The diagonals cut each other in ——— . [a fraction]

2. Calculate the size of each missing angle in each parallelogram:

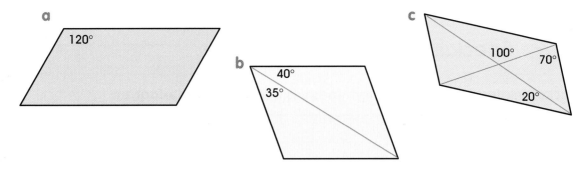

3. Calculate the missing sides and perimeter (where needed) of each parallelogram:

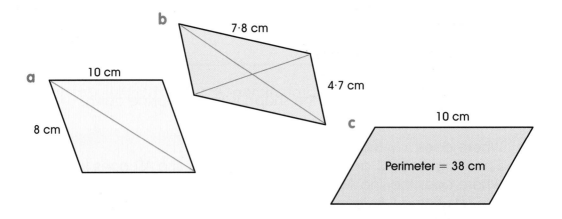

4. Name the other quadrilaterals that also have half-turn symmetry (and are therefore special parallelograms).

7 Circles: Diameter and Circumference

Circumference

Radius

Diameter

Centre

There is a connection between the radius and the diameter:

Diameter = 2 × Radius

The **circumference** is the distance round a circle.

Is there a connection between the diameter and the circumference?

A

1. a   Make a collection of five circular objects.
        For each one, measure the diameter and the circumference.
    b   Collect your data in a table like this:

Object	1	2	3	4	5
Diameter					
Circumference					
C ÷ D					

    c   Check that in each case the circumference is roughly three times the diameter.

        Can you be more accurate?

2. Find a rough estimate of the circumference of each circle using the formula C = 3D:

a
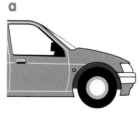

b

c

d

e

D = 500 cm   D = 3 cm   D = 12 mm   D = 220 cm   D = 8000 miles

3. Estimate the size of the circumference when the radius is:

    a   10 cm   b   25 cm   c   300 mm   d   17 mm.

Unit 22 Ratio

Two thirds of the world is ocean

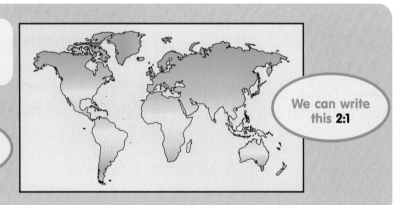

This means that 2 parts in 3 is ocean and 1 part in 3 is land.

We say the **ratio** of sea to land is 2 to 1

We can write this **2:1**

1 Looking Back

1. Copy and complete each equation, forming equivalent fractions:

   a $\frac{1}{2} = \frac{3}{?}$ b $\frac{2}{3} = \frac{?}{27}$ c $\frac{3}{4} = \frac{15}{?}$ d $\frac{3}{5} = \frac{18}{?}$ e $\frac{25}{100} = \frac{?}{4}$

2. Express each fraction in its simplest form:

   a $\frac{25}{50}$ b $\frac{35}{40}$ c $\frac{40}{60}$ d $\frac{80}{120}$ e $\frac{250}{400}$

   f $\frac{240}{360}$ g $\frac{75}{100}$ h $\frac{32}{96}$ i $\frac{90}{150}$ j $\frac{150}{350}$

3. a In a box of jelly beans, there were 150 sweets. 40 of them were red.
   What fraction of the sweets were red?

   b Jane got 60 cards on her birthday.
   25 of the cards had a badge saying 'You are 11'.
   What fraction of the cards had badges?

4. The population of Upper Mulch is 2400. When the local rugby team
   reached the final, $\frac{3}{8}$ of the population bought tickets for the match.
   How many people was this?

5. Calculate each amount. Remember to include the units in your answers.

   a $\frac{3}{5}$ of 1 m   b $\frac{4}{5}$ of 3 kg   c $\frac{3}{5}$ of 1 litre   d $\frac{3}{4}$ of £3   e $\frac{9}{10}$ of 1 cm
   f $\frac{2}{3}$ of £468   g $\frac{2}{7}$ of £44·45   h $\frac{9}{25}$ of £24·75   i $\frac{19}{20}$ of £7   j $\frac{23}{50}$ of £17·50

2 Something New: Ratio

On a school outing to the theatre, the rules say that there must be one adult for every ten children.

If there are 40 children, there must be four adults.
Adults:children = 4:40 = 1:10   These are **equivalent ratios**.
1:10 is the **simplest form**.

Ratios can be written in the form of a fraction.
1:10 = $\frac{1}{10}$ = 0·1   The number of adults is one tenth of the number of children.

Note that the **order** is important – 1:10 is not the same as 10:1.
10:1 = $\frac{10}{1}$ = 10   The number of children is ten times the number of adults.

Ratio is used to compare quantities:
Both parts of the ratio should be in the same units.

Example   Express the ratio 5p to £2 in its simplext form.

First, put them in the same units.   5p:£2 = 5p:200p
= 5:200
Divide both sides by 5.   = 1:40

 A

1. Express each of the following as a ratio in its simplest form:

a 2:4	b 3:6	c 4:12	d 5:20	e 6:24
f 10:50	g 12:36	h 50:150	i 50:75	j 20:120
k 6:30	l 35:15	m 18:12	n 36:9	o 81:21

2. Express each of the following ratios as a fraction in its simplest form:

a 10:30	b 10:25	c 4:16	d 3:9	e 2:12
f 15:50	g 9:27	h 9:36	i 40:100	j 50:125
k 80:20	l 42:14	m 30:18	n 99:11	o 52:13

3. The school secretary collected the numbers of girls and boys in each class. She started working out the ratio of girls:boys and girls:pupils for each class.

   a Copy and complete the table below:

Class	Girls	Boys	Girls:Boys	Girls:Pupils
P1	12	15	12:15 = 4:5	12:27 = 4:9
P2	18	9	2:1	2:3
P3	16	12	4:3	
P4	10	18		
P5	14	16		
P6	13	12		
P7	9	15		

   b Use the information above to find, for the whole school, the ratio of:
   i girls:boys ii girls:pupils

4. At a zoo, there are 200 penguins, 40 monkeys and 10 camels.

   a Express the following ratios in their simplest terms:
   i camels:monkeys
   ii penguins:camels
   iii monkeys:penguins
   iv monkeys:camels

   b For this group of animals work out the ratio:
   i birds:other animals
   ii two-legged:four-legged

   c The camel has a single hump,
   The dromedary two;
   Or else the other way around.
   I'm never sure. Are you?

   Ogden Nash

   Of the ten camels, four were dromedaries and the rest were bactrian (two humped).

   Express as a ratio in its simplest form:
   i dromedaries:camels ii bactrians:dromedaries

5. Write down the following ratios in their simplest form.
   Remember The quantities must be in the same units.

   a 50p:£1   b 20p:£1   c 10p:£2   d 2p:£20
   e 1p:£1   f 50 g:1 kg   g 300 g:2 kg   h 40 g:320 g
   i 750 g:3 kg   j 1 kg:1 tonne   k 10 ml:1 litre   l 250 ml:3 litre
   m 5 ml:5 litre   n 12 litres:240 ml

B

1. Express these ratios of coins in their simplest terms.
   Remember The order is also important.

   a 25p:5p   b 5p:25p   c 2p:10p   d 10p:50p   e 50p:10p

2. A gardener plans a new garden.
   He measures the heights of different plants.

   A Foxtail lily 2·8 m
   B Japanese anemone 1·2 m
   C Delphinium 1 m
   D Iris 70 cm
   E Peony 60 cm

   Express the ratios of heights of the plants in their simplest terms:

   a C:B   b C:D   c D:E   d E:C   e C:E
   f A:B   g B:A   h B:E   i A:E   j B:C

3. The printer has blurred some of the numbers in the following ratios.
   Copy and complete the table:

Ratio	30:60	40:120	75:50	125:175	250:120	16:36	48:40
Simplest form	1:⬦	⬦:3	3:⬦	5:⬦	⬦:12	4:⬦	6:⬦

4. Express each of the following ratios in its simplest form:

   a 6 cm:24 cm   b 250 g:1 kg   c 1·5 m:50 cm   d 100 ml:1 litre

5. A traffic census at a school found that 60 children
   walked to school and 180 came by car. This
   accounted for all the children in the school.

   a Express the number of children who walked to the
      number who came by car as a ratio in the simplest form.

   b i   How many children attended the school?
      ii Express the number of children who walked to the number in the
          school as a ratio in the simplest form.

3 Working with Ratio

A

1. In the local nursery the ratio adults:children = 1:8.

   a If there are 40 children, how many adults are there?
   b If there are 6 adults, how many children are there?

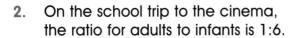

2. On the school trip to the cinema,
   the ratio for adults to infants is 1:6.

   a If there were nine adults, how many infants are there?
   b 72 infants want to see the movie *Elf*. If the ratio adults:infants
      is kept to 1:6, how many adults are required?

3. For safety reasons, it was decided that science classes with one teacher
   could only have 15 pupils in them.

   a Express the number of teachers to pupils as a ratio.
   b In first year, there are 150 pupils. How many classes
      will there have to be for science?
   c On Monday, there are eight science teachers in school.
      How many pupils can they teach science to at the same time?

4. When making biscuits, the ratio of sugar to flour was 1:4.

   a If 120 g of flour is used, how much sugar is
      needed?
   b James used 50 g of sugar to make his batch
      of biscuits. How much flour did he use?

B

1. Six children were saving for a school trip. Sue's father agreed that for every
   £1 she saved, he would give her £4. Sue's share:father's share = 1:4.
   The other five children made similar deals with their parents.
   The table gives the ratios:

   a Sue, Peter and Ben each saved £10.
      Calculate what their parents gave them.
   b Andrew's parents gave him £42. How much
      had he saved?
   c Emma's parents gave her £40. How much
      had she saved?
   d In total, Belinda ended up with £66. Was this
      because she saved £5, £6 or £7?

Name	Share Ratio
Sue	1:4
Peter	1:5
Ben	1:3
Andrew	1:6
Emma	1:2
Belinda	1:10

2. The builders mix sand and cement together to make concrete.
   The ratio of sand to cement is 3:1.

   a How much cement is needed if 342 kg
   of sand is used?
   b If instead, 125 kg of cement is used,
   how much sand is needed?
   c A batch of concrete weighing 332 kg is
   mixed.

   Does this contain 81, 82, 83, 84 or 85 kg of cement?

3. Jack made a purple paint by mixing red with blue in the ratio 3:1.

   a If he uses 18 litres of red, how much blue
   is needed?
   b If he has 24 litres of red and 10 litres of
   blue, what is the largest amount of purple
   he can make?
   c If he has 30 litres of red and 9 litres of
   blue, what is the largest amount of purple
   he can make?

4 Model Making

When you make a model, the scale is often quoted as a ratio.
Measurement on model:measurement in real life

Example   A model car has a scale of 1:20.

              The length of the model is 18 cm.
              What is the length of the real thing?
              18 × 20 = 360 cm

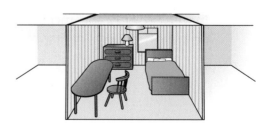

A

1. Keiko received doll's house furniture for her Christmas present.
   The toy furniture is made to a scale of 1:20.

   a A model table is 6 cm long.
   How long is the real table in:
   i cm   ii m?

   b A model chair was 4 cm high.
   How high was the actual chair in:
   i cm   ii m?

c   Actual drawers are 60 cm wide.
    How wide are model drawers in:
    i cm   ii mm?

d   A real bed is 1·6 m long.
    How long is a model bed in:
    i cm   and   ii mm?

2. A designer is making a model village to a scale of 1:40.

    a   On the model, the museum to the town hall is 240 cm.
        What is the real-life distance in:
        i cm   ii m?

    b   The distance from the museum to the science dome is 200 m.
        What distance is this represented by in the model?
    c   The museum to the church is 1·6 m on the model.
        How far apart are they in real life?

3. A toy manufacturer makes model cars, all to the same scale.
    The table gives some details:

Colour	Model Size (cm)	Actual Size (m)
Blue	25	2
Green		2·4
Red	20	
Black		1·6
White	24	

    a   Use the information about the blue car to work out the scale as a ratio.
    b   Use the ratio to help you copy and complete the table.

4. The front of a public building is 80·1 m long.
    A model is made that is 178 cm long.

    a   Calculate the scale of the model.
    b   The main doors are 2·5 m tall.
        How tall are the model doors?
    c   The first floor of the model is 14 cm high.
        How high is the real first floor?

Unit 23 Sequences

Sequences arise in the strangest situations

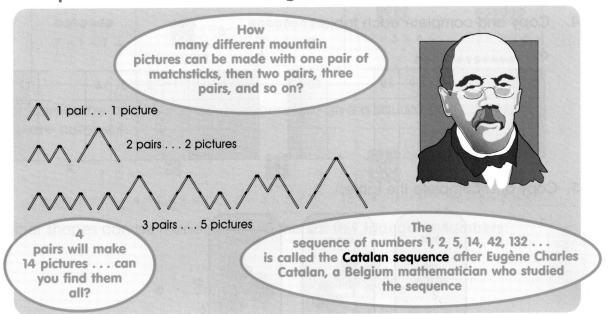

How many different mountain pictures can be made with one pair of matchsticks, then two pairs, three pairs, and so on?

1 pair . . . 1 picture

2 pairs . . . 2 pictures

3 pairs . . . 5 pictures

4 pairs will make 14 pictures . . . can you find them all?

The sequence of numbers 1, 2, 5, 14, 42, 132 . . . is called the **Catalan sequence** after Eugène Charles Catalan, a Belgium mathematician who studied the sequence

1 Looking Back

1. Find the next three terms in each of these sequences.
    Write a sentence describing the rule that you used.

    a   3, 7, 11, 15, ___, ___, ___   b   1, 3, 9, 27, ___, ___, ___
    c   1, 1, 2, 3, 5, 8, ___, ___, ___   d   95, 89, 83, 77, ___, ___, ___

2.

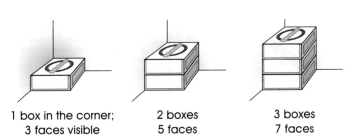

1 box in the corner;   2 boxes   3 boxes
3 faces visible   5 faces   7 faces

    a   List the next three numbers in the sequence: 3, 5, 7, ___, ___, ___
    b   Which of the following formulae will give the number of visible faces (F) when there are *n* boxes in the corner?
        i F = 2n − 1   ii F = 2n + 1   iii F = 3n + 1

Challenge

Which of these sequences has 1000 as one of its terms?

a 1, 4, 7, 10, ...   b 10, 16, 22, 28, ...
c 6, 13, 20, 27, ...   d 21, 32, 43, 54, 65 ...

Hint In each case find the *n*th term formula then use it to find if 1000 is one of the terms.

4 Which One?

Example   The sequence 2, 5, 8, 11, ... has *n*th term = 3*n* – 1.
What position does 65 take up in the sequence?

$$3n - 1 = 65$$
so $3n = 66$
so $n = 22$
65 is the 22nd term in the sequence.

  A

1. a The sequence 5, 9, 13, ... has *n*th term = 4*n* + 1.
       Where is 49 in the sequence?
    b The sequence 3, 10, 17, ... has *n*th term = 7*n* – 4.
       Where is 136 in the sequence?
    c The sequence 100, 92, 84, ... has *n*th term = 108 – 8*n*.
       Where is 12 in the sequence?

2. For each sequence:
    i state the *n*th term   ii work out the position of the extra term:

    a 5, 15, 25, ... , 95   b 12, 17, 22, 27, ... , 102
    c 4, 16, 28, ... , 100   d 3, 9, 15, 21, ... , 105

3. a Form a sequence using
       the matchstick patterns.
    b State a formula for the
       *n*th term.
    c Which pattern requires
       39 matches to build?

        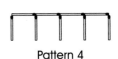

    Pattern 1   Pattern 2   Pattern 3   Pattern 4

4. Which pattern in this
    sequence of pictures will
    need 105 matches to build?

    1   2   3   4

Unit 24 — Information Handling

The **average** is what we consider to be typical or usual for a situation

The TV programme **2 point 4 children** was so called because that was considered to be the average number of children in a family

Recently it was found that average family size is no longer 2·4 children but 1·64

1 ▶ Looking Back

1. This table gives information on 20 islands in Scotland.

   a If a database had been created using this data:
      i how many fields would make up the database
      ii how many records would be listed in the database?

   b The island records are already sorted. Which field are they sorted by and in which order (ascending or descending)?

Island	Pop'n	Area (ha)
Lewis with Harris	21 680	222 500
Orkney Mainland	17 560	58 308
Shetland Mainland	15 120	100 230
Skye	8840	166 500
Bute, Island of	7350	12 217
Arran	4470	43 201
Islay	3538	61 950
Mull	2680	87 794
South Uist	2285	32 026
North Uist	1815	30 305
Benbecula	1800	8203
Great Cumbrae	1393	1168
Barra	1315	6835
Yell	1083	21 211
Unst	1067	12 068
Whalsay	1043	1970
South Ronaldsay	943	4980
West Burra	817	743
Tiree	768	7834

If you have access to a computer, create a database using the islands information.

   c Sort the records by area in ascending order.
     i Which is the largest island listed?
     ii Which is the smallest island listed?

   d Search the records to find the island with a population of 1067 people.

2. This table provides information on eight of Scotland's lochs.

   a A database is to be created using this data.
     i Name the fields making up the database.
     ii Name the two field types used.

   b The lochs records are already sorted. Which field are they sorted by and in which order?

   c Suggest one more field heading for the database.

Loch	Depth (m)	Area (ha)
Loch Tay	155	2642
Loch Shiel	128	1968
Loch Rannoch	134	1917
Loch Ness	230	5672
Loch Morar	337	2668
Loch Maree	112	2849
Loch Lomond	190	7100
Loch Katrine	151	1238

If you have access to a computer, create a database using the lochs information.

   d Sort the records by depth in **ascending order**.
     i Which is the deepest listed?
     ii Which is the most shallow loch listed?

   e Search the records to find the loch with an area of 5672 ha.

3. The records shown provide information on exercises completed at a circuit training class.

	John	Lynn	Kevin	Beth	George	Drew
Sit-ups	50	60	25	35	40	30
Press-ups	25	12	25	20	15	20
Squat thrusts	40	40	25	50	35	50
Pull-ups	10	10	15	10	10	20
Total	125	122	90	115	100	120

These records are stored in a database.

a What are the six fields making up the database?
b What are the two field types making up the database?
c Who completed the highest number of:
   i   sit-ups
   ii pull-ups?

d The database is sorted by name in ascending order.
   Draw the sorted database records using a list layout.

2 Interpreting a Database

1. The data table provides information on ten of Scotland's stadiums and
    arenas.

Stadium/Arena	Opened	Capacity	Location
Meadowbank	1969	15 000	Edinburgh
Murrayfield	1925	67 500	Edinburgh
Tannadice	1909	14 209	Dundee
The National Stadium	1903	52 000	Glasgow
Pittodrie	1903	21 634	Aberdeen
Easter Road Park	1880	17 500	Edinburgh
Ibrox	1873	50 411	Glasgow
Tynecastle	1886	18 008	Edinburgh
Braehead	1999	4000	Glasgow
Parkhead	1888	60 424	Glasgow

a Which of the stadiums was built before 1900 **and** has a capacity less
   than 18 000?
b Which of the stadiums were built after 1900 **and** have a capacity more
   than 20 000?
c Name the stadiums with a capacity greater than 55 000 **or** which were
   built in 1880.
d Name the stadiums which were opened in 1909 **or** have a capacity
   less than 10 000.
e Name the two stadiums which were **not** built before 1939.
f Name the six stadiums which were **not** built before 1901.

2. The table provides information on the properties of solids:

Shape	Faces	Edges	Vertices
Cube	6	12	8
Cylinder	3	2	0
Sphere	1	0	0
Cuboid	6	12	8
Square-based pyramid	5	8	5
Tetrahedron	4	6	4
Triangular prism	5	9	6

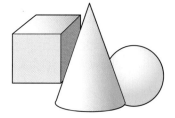

a Which of the shapes have less than six edges **and** vertices?
b Name the shapes which have more than six vertices **or** four faces.
c Which shape has more than eight edges **and** five faces?
d Which shape does **not** have at least one edge?
e Extend the database by adding details of any other solid shapes
   you know.

3. The data table provides details
   of school clothing orders at the
   beginning of term:

Class	T-shirts	Sweatshirts	Ties
Primary 1	27	26	24
Primary 2	20	20	8
Primary 3	17	16	6
Primary 4	21	22	4
Primary 5	22	18	2
Primary 6	26	21	0
Primary 7	19	19	1

a In which classes are there less
   than 7 ties **and** more than 20
   T-shirts ordered?
b Which classes are **not**
   ordering more than 20
   sweatshirts?
c Which classes have ordered
   more than 25 T-shirts **or** sweatshirts?
d Which class has ordered less than 20 T-shirts, less than 20 sweatshirts
   and more than 5 ties?

If you have access to a computer, create databases
from the tables in questions **1** to **3**.

Use the **Match Records** facility to find the answers
to the questions.

> = means **greater than or equal to**.

< = means **less than or equal to**.

B

1. The table shows the distance travelled in a week by a driver from Parcel Fast Deliveries:

Journey	Distance (km)	Duration (min)	Cost (£)
Glasgow – Edinburgh	79·5	60	£16·69
Edinburgh – Perth	66·3	49	
Perth – Glasgow	103·5	75	
Glasgow – Irvine	41·5	43	
Irvine – Ayr	19·2	18	
Ayr – Glasgow	58·7	50	
Glasgow – Kingussie	214·8	175	
Kingussie – Aviemore	19·6	18	
Aviemore – Glasgow	230·9	191	
Glasgow – Galashiels	127·3	100	
Galashiels – Glasgow	127·3	100	
Total			

The van uses 21p of petrol for every kilometre driven.

a Complete the **Cost (£)** column of the table.
b Complete the **Total** row.
c Where do you think the driver is based?
d The journeys are listed in the order driven and were made from Monday to Thursday.
  Monday's route: Glasgow to Perth via Edinburgh and return.
  Give the routes for the other three days.
e Which day did the driver go straight to his final destination of the day, with no stops?
f Which of the journeys was longer than 2 hours and further than 220 km?
g Name the journeys less than or equal to 58·7 km long.
h Which journeys were shorter than 60 km and took 43 minutes or less?
i Which journeys were less than 50 km long or cost £13·92 or less?

If you have access to a computer, create a database using the journeys information.
Do not include the totals.
Use the **Match Records** facility to find the answers to questions **f–h**.

The Mean

The **mean** is one type of average.
We work out the mean of a set of data by finding the **sum** of the pieces
of data and **dividing it by** the number of pieces of data.

1. **a** Find the mean height of a school football team where the heights
       of the players are:
       1·6 m, 1·5 m, 1·5 m, 1·4 m, 1·3 m, 1·4 m,
       1·4 m, 1·3 m, 1·5 m, 1·3 m, 1·6 m
    b The total weight of ten bags of sweets is 1830 g.
       What is the mean weight?
    c The shoe sizes of 20 pupils add up to 60. What is the mean shoe size?
    d What is the mean cost of a DVD when nine DVDs cost £109·91?
    e What is the mean test score if the combined score is 2112 for a class
       of 23 children?

2. **a** What is the mean length of these Scottish canals?

Caledonian Canal 96 km	Forth and Clyde Canal 56 km
Union Canal 51 km	Aberdeenshire Canal 29 km
Monkland Canal 19 km	Glasgow, Paisley Canal 17 km
Crinan Canal 14 km	Spynie Canal 10 km

    b What is the mean runway length of these Scottish airports?

Campbeltown Airport 3049 m	Prestwick Airport 2987 m
Glasgow Airport 2658 m	Edinburgh Airport 2560 m
Aberdeen Airport 1829 m	Benbecula Airport 1681 m
Dundee Airport 1400 m	Oban Airport 1125 m
Tobermory Airport 800 m	Colonsay Airport 505 m

    c Find the mean weight of a cake.

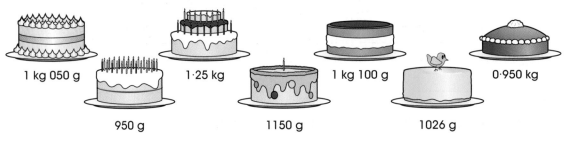

1 kg 050 g   1·25 kg   1 kg 100 g   0·950 kg

950 g   1150 g   1026 g

d What is the mean volume of liquid in a container?

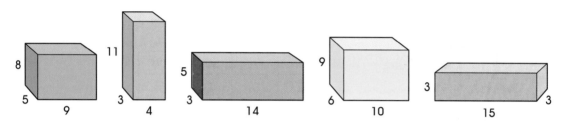

e Calculate the mean volume of a cuboid. All measurements are in centimetres.

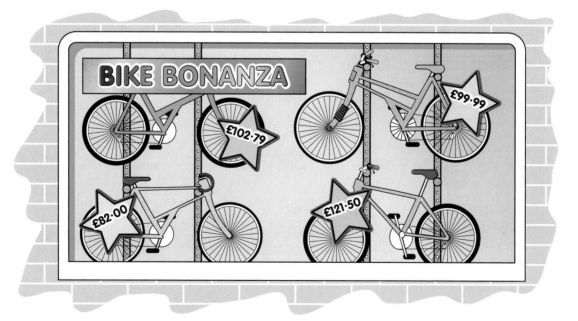

3. Mary is looking into the price of bikes.
At Supercycles, she notes the following prices:
£106·50, £110·00, £92·99, £89·50.
Looking in the window at Bike Bonanza she sees the same bikes at different prices.

Which shop sells the cheapest bikes on average?

◆ **Investigate**

What is the mean number of pages in a block (7 Units) of this book?

   a   Design a table to record your data.
   b   Collect the data on the number of pages in each block.

   Hint If a block starts on page 50 and finishes on page 112 it has
         112 − 50 + 1 = 63 pages.

   c   Use the data to find the mean number of pages in a block.

B

1.   The table records the amount of rainfall each day for
       the month of February:

	Mon	Tue	Wed	Thu	Fri	Sat	Sun
Week 1	0	4	3	2	0	0	6
Week 2	5	3	0	2	0	5	7
Week 3	8	6	3	1	0	3	3
Week 4	4	0	0	2	0	2	6

   a   What was the mean daily rainfall in
      i Week 1   ii Week 2   iii Week 3   iv Week 4?

   b   What was the mean rainfall on a:
      i Monday   ii Tuesday   iii Thursday   iv Sunday?

   c   What was the mean daily rainfall in the month of February?
   d   What was the mean weekly rainfall in the month of February?

2.   Here are eight little spiders, but one has lost a leg.

   a   Find the mean number of legs per spider.
   b   Why would it be better to say the average number of legs on a spider
      is eight?

Unit 25 Decimals

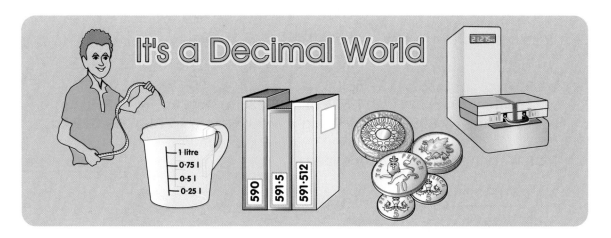

It's a Decimal World

1 Looking Back

1. Here is a number line that shows the units broken into thousandths (0·001).

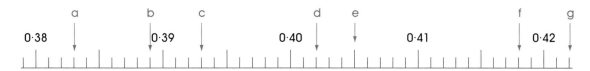

Arrow **a** points to **0·383**.
Write in decimal form the number to which each of the other arrows point.

2. In the number 84·87, the blue digit is worth 7 hundredths or 0·07.
In the number 10·099, the blue digit is worth 9 thousandths or 0·009.

In a similar way, write the value of each blue digit in the following numbers:

a 89·567   b 9·083   c 121·08
d 240·78   e 7·007   f 68·085

3. 4·078 is written in words as *four and seventy-eight thousandths.*
15·365 is written in words as *fifteen and three hundred and sixty-five thousandths.*

Write the following in words:

a 1·005   b 25·074   c 33·303   d 60·060   e 56·200   f 60·51

4. *Twelve point four six one*, written as a number is 12·461.
   Write these as numbers:

   a eight point one nine five   b fifty point zero two four
   c eleven point nine zero one   d seven point zero zero two

5. Write out each list in order, smallest first:

   a 1·897   0·756   0·026   3·365   1·969   0·881
   b 55·8   5·787   55·08   15·78   0·578   5·877
   c 18·44 m   18·8 m   1·878 m   8·338 m   18 m   8·787 m
   d 90·09 kg   9·009 kg   19·99 kg   9·909 kg   99·99 kg   9·099 kg

6. Match each label with a container:

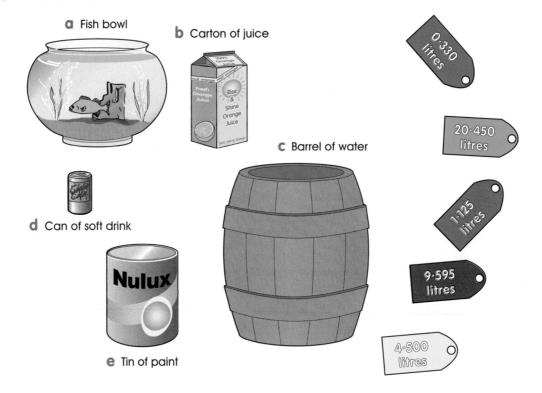

a Fish bowl
b Carton of juice
c Barrel of water
d Can of soft drink
e Tin of paint

Nulux

0·330 litres
20·450 litres
1·125 litres
9·595 litres
4·500 litres

2 Round and Round

A

1. Round each of these numbers to 1 decimal place:

   a 23·28   b 49·74   c 6·895   d 165·39
   e 200·11   f 67·949   g 9·984

2. Add or subtract the following pairs of numbers.
   Round your answers to 1 decimal place.

   a 18·17 + 28·74   **b** 71·74 − 16·05   **c** 89·92 + 90·5
   d 64 − 39·65   **e** 86·68 + 19·86   **f** 90 − 44·12

3. **Estimate** the answer to each calculation by rounding the data to
   1 decimal place.

   Example   15·254 + 7·427 is about 15·3 + 7·4, which is 22·7.

      a 9·223 + 8·662   **b** 20·544 − 9·253   **c** 19·447 + 9·961
      d 31·869 − 7·744   **e** 35·435 − 12·358   **f** 28·571 + 10·416

4. At Albion Primary's Fun Day, there was a
   competition to see who could throw a
   beanbag the furthest distance.
   Each person was given two attempts.
   The top four results are shown here:

   Find the winner of the competition by
   rounding each throw to 1 decimal
   place and **estimating** the total of each person's attempts.

	1st Attempt	2nd Attempt
Zahid	14·56 m	15·22 m
Nina	12·45 m	16·55 m
Gordon	17·81 m	15·19 m
Jean	16·56 m	14·54 m

Challenge

Five friends went on holiday taking
one suitcase each with them.
Margaret and Elspeth's suitcases had
a combined weight of about 30·5 kg.
Derek's suitcase weighed about 2·6 kg
more than John's. The difference between
the weight of Colin and Margaret's
suitcases was about ½ kg.

Which suitcase belongs to each person?

a 16·895 kg
b 17·354 kg
c 16·448 kg
d 19·981 kg
e 14·146 kg

3   Multiplying and Dividing by 10, 100 and 1000

 A

1. Calculate:

   a 22·17 × 10   **b** 7·09 × 100   **c** 15·15 × 1000   **d** 500·1 ÷ 10
   e 2·7 ÷ 100   **f** 9·06 × 100   **g** 8 ÷ 1000   **h** 52·5 × 1000
   i 70·6 ÷ 100   **j** 39·009 × 100   **k** 404 ÷ 1000   **l** 144·4 ÷ 100
   m 9·005 × 1000   **n** 7·007 × 100   **o** 5000 ÷ 1000

9.

a Grant took advantage of Fab Fashions' special **3 T-shirts for the price of 2** offer and bought six for his holidays. How much did he pay?

b Adele saved a fifth on her trainers. What was the original cost?

• FAB FASHIONS •

T-shirt
£12·79

Hooded top
£14·48

Trainers
£63

Cap
£5·95

 Challenge

The shop made £120 one Saturday morning with the sale of hooded tops and caps. How many of each were bought?

B

1. Calculate:

   a 3·25 + 4·687   b 5·926 + 1·09   c 8·15 − 3·061
   d 5 + 3·22 + 4·078 e 4·4 − 2·727   f 7·3 + 0·587 + 2·66
   g 9 − 5·237   h 3·33 + 2·9 + 4

2. Add or subtract decimals **mentally**:

   a 15·4 + 14·5   b 22·6 + 13·3   c 24·6 − 16·2   d 30·3 − 17·1
   e 15·4 + 17·5   f 8·5 + 6·3 + 4·1   g 52·8 − 13·5   h 11·6 + 9·2 + 8·2
   i 20 − 8·3   j 50 − 22·6

3. Mrs Spencer made two new shelves from a piece of wood that was 3·6 metres long.

   If one shelf was 1·345 m and the other was 1·58 m, how much wood was left over?

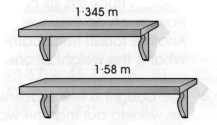

1·345 m

1·58 m

4. **a** Find the total weight of these three gifts.
   b Work out the difference between the
   largest and smallest gifts.

5. Calculate:

   a 68·78 × 6   **b** 95·06 × 9   **c** 325 ÷ 4   **d** 461·1 ÷ 5
   e 7·782 × 8   **f** 5·909 × 7   **g** 8·208 ÷ 8   **h** 3·312 ÷ 9
   i (124 ÷ 8) × 9 **j** (1·236 × 7) ÷ 4

6. A special pack of nine bottles of Mountain Spring water have a total
   volume of 11·475 litres.

   a Work out the volume of one bottle.
   b Round your answer to 1 decimal place.

7. Returning home from France, Claire had £6 worth of euro left, Patrick had
   £7 worth, Ross had £9 worth and Tammy had £6 worth.
   If £1 = €1·57, calculate the average amount of euro they had left.

Challenge

The Larriot Hotel
£32·48 per person per night

The Milton Hotel
£49·79 per person per night

Children half price

4 nights for the price of 3

   a Mr and Mrs Peters stayed at The Larriot Hotel at Euro Disney with
   their two children.
   They were given a bill for £292·32.
   How many nights did they stay?
   b Mr and Mrs Mullan stayed for ten nights at The Milton Hotel. Find
   the cost of their stay.

5 Calculator Work

A

1. Calculate the difference in total volume between the:

   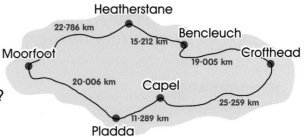

   a blue and yellow containers
   b yellow and red containers
   c blue and red containers.

2. a Adam bought a new computer for £899·99,
      a printer for £109·79 and a digital camera for £149·45.
      How much did he spend altogether?
   b Kate bought exactly the same as Adam in another shop for a special
      price of £999·99. How much money did she save?

3. James drove from Moorfoot to
   Crofthead via Pladda and
   Capel. Shannon went via
   Heatherstane and Bencleuch.

   a Who had the shortest journey?
   b By how many kilometres?

   Heatherstane
   22·786 km
   15·212 km
   Bencleuch
   Moorfoot
   Crofthead
   19·005 km
   20·006 km
   Capel
   25·259 km
   11·289 km
   Pladda

4. Calculate:

   a $(55·207 - 18·253) + 27·707$ b $(90·099 - 25·289) + 8·085$
   c $(213·25 \times 65) \div 50$ d $(1860·76 \div 200) \times 90$

5. A box of chocolates weighs 0·475 kg. Work out the weight of:

   a 25   b 144   c 250   d 400 boxes.

6. Mr Smith, a taxi driver, drove 7087·65 km during the month of June.

   a Calculate the average amount of kilometres he travelled per day.
   b Round your answer to 1 decimal place.

Challenge

Chris added four of
these numbers together.
He then multiplied the
answer by the
remaining number.
His answer was 60 002.
How did he get this answer?

Volume and Weight

The metric system we use today was developed in the late 18th century in France

The mathematician in charge was an Italian called Joseph Lagrange. Under the system, the prefixes (starts) of words can have an important meaning.

Milli- means **one thousandth** part. A millilitre is a thousandth part of a litre

Kilo- means a **thousand** parts. A kilogram is a thousand grams

1 Looking Back

1. How many millilitres are there in:

    a $\frac{1}{2}$ litre   b $\frac{3}{4}$ litre   c $\frac{2}{5}$ litre   d $\frac{1}{100}$ litre?

2. How many millilitres of liquid are in each container?

    a   b   c   d

3. Write these volumes in millilitres:

    a 8 litres   b 3·5 litres   c $5\frac{1}{4}$ litres   d 7·1 litres
    e 36 litres   f $18\frac{4}{5}$ litres   g 6·75 litres   h 14·05 litres

4. Write these volumes using millilitres only:

    a 9 litres 450 ml   b 12 litres 608 ml   c 10 litres 80 ml

5. Write these volumes in litres and millilitres:

   a 7400 ml   b 8035 ml   c 3·625 ml   d 15·8 litres   e 9·06 litres

6. Write these volumes in litres only:

   a 1850 ml   b 14 250 ml   c 26 700 ml   d 5050 ml   e 815 ml

7. a How many **litres** of the punch are made
      from the recipe to serve 12?
   b 72 guests are coming to the
      party.

      How many litres of:
      i   apple juice
      ii orange juice
      iii ginger ale
      are needed to serve the guests with Party Punch?

   c How many litres of Party Punch are needed for the 72 guests?

1 cm³ is 1/1000 of a litre = 1 millilitre = 1 ml.

8. a Each edge of this cube is 1 cm long.
      What is the volume of the cube?
   b Copy and complete:
      ___ cm³ = 1 litre.

9. This cube is made from lots of centimetre cubes.

   a How many rows of cm cubes are in the
      bottom layer?
   b How many cm cubes are in a row?
   c How many cm cubes fill the bottom layer?
   d How many of these layers are there in the
      cube?
   e How many cm cubes are needed to make
      the cube?
   f What is the volume of the cube?

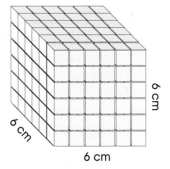

6 cm
6 cm
6 cm

10. Use the steps in question **9** above to help you find how many centimetre
    cubes would fill each of these cuboids:

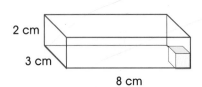

2 cm
3 cm
8 cm

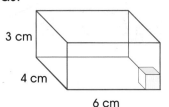

3 cm
4 cm
6 cm

11. What is the volume of each cuboid in question **10**?

12. Change these weights into grams:

| a 7·136 kg | b 11·514 kg | c 0·825 kg | d 0·4 kg | e 6·05 kg |

13. Change these weights into kilograms:

| a 2819 grams | b 10 050 grams | c 670 grams | d 47 grams |

14. Write these weights in kilograms and grams:

| a 4·518 kg | b 18·3 kg | c 7·04 kg | d 1050 grams | e 8063 grams |

15. The maximum weight that is safe in this lift is 300 kg.

Five people are waiting for the lift:
Adam, who weighs $67\frac{1}{2}$ kg
Bob, 73 kg 670 g
Colin, $73\frac{3}{4}$ kg
Dave, 61 kg 800 g
Eric, 73·7 kg.

a Is it safe to carry all five men in the lift? Explain.
b Who is the heaviest?
c Does it matter which four travel in the lift?

16. The Crumble Crisp company makes a batch of 120 kilograms of crisps.
The crisps are put into airtight packets, each containing 25 g.

a How many of the packets can be filled?
b The packets are sold at 30 pence each.
How much is made from the sale of all the crisps?

2 Heavyweight!

1000 milligrams = 1 gram

1000 grams = 1 kilogram

1000 kilograms = 1 tonne

1 gram is the weight of 1 cm³ of water.

1 kg is the weight of 1 litre (1000 cm³) of water.

1 tonne is the weight of 1000 litres (1 m³) of water.

A

1. Which unit would you use to weigh:

   a a bus   **b** a bag of potatoes   **c** a golf ball
   d an aeroplane   **e** a heavy suitcase   **f** yourself
   g a bar of chocolate   **h** the water in a swimming pool?

2. Change these weights into kilograms:

   a 3·178 tonnes   **b** 12·065 tonnes
   c 5 tonnes 275 kg   **d** 2 tonnes 55 kg

3. Change these weights into tonnes:

   a 4635 kg   **b** 10 050 kg   **c** 625 kg   **d** 100 kg   **e** 5 kg

4. Express these weights in tonnes and kilograms:

   a 7·2 tonnes   **b** 12·6 tonnes   **c** 4·05 tonnes
   d 15·08 tonnes   **e** 0·63 tonnes

5. Lorries are weighed before and after being loaded. For each lorry, calculate:
   i its weight in tonnes
   ii the weight of its load.

   > **Hint** You must multiply the reading by 100 to get the weight in kilograms.

a

b
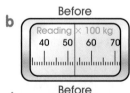

c

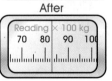

d
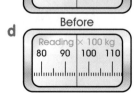
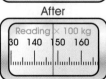

6. a A lorry with a four tonne load of timber delivers 675 kg of the timber.
       What weight of timber remains?
    b The lorry then delivers 860 kg, and then 585 kg of the timber.
       How much of the four tonne load now remains?

7. A lorry delivers eight loads of granite chips.
    Each load is 6 tonnes 375 kg.
    Calculate the total weight of granite chips
    delivered.

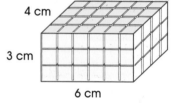

8. Farmer Jones had six fields growing potatoes this year.
    The total yield from the six fields was $87\frac{1}{2}$ tonnes.
    Calculate the average yield per field, to the nearest 100 kg.

3 The Volume of a Cuboid

1. The cuboid is made up of 1 cm cubes.

    a How many rows of cubes are there on the
       bottom layer?
    b How many cubes in each row?
    c How many cubes in the bottom layer?
    d How many layers are there?
    e How many 1 cm cubes in total make up
       the cuboid?
    f What is the volume of the cuboid?

2. a Write down:
       i   the length
       ii   the breadth
       iii the height of the cuboid in question **1**.

    b Check that the volume is equal to **length × breadth × height**.

Volume = number of cm cubes in a row × number of rows × number of layers
        = **length** (cm)   × **breadth** (cm) × **height** (cm).

For any cuboid, the volume is $V = l \times b \times h$ or $V = lbh$

The units of l, b and h must all be the same.

---

3. Use the formula *V* = *lbh* to calculate the volume of each cuboid:

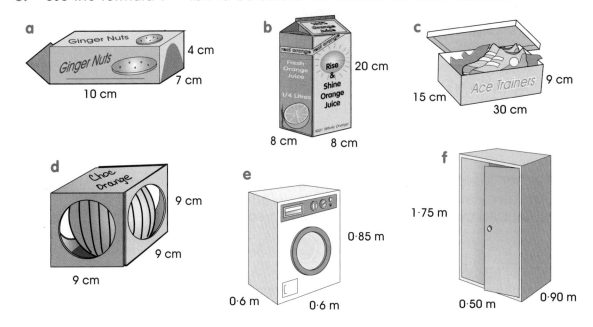

a Ginger Nuts
4 cm
7 cm
10 cm

b 20 cm
8 cm   8 cm

c Ace Trainers
9 cm
15 cm
30 cm

d Choc Orange
9 cm
9 cm
9 cm

e 0·85 m
0·6 m   0·6 m

f 1·75 m
0·50 m   0·90 m

4. Calculate the volume of each object. **Hint** Be careful with the units!

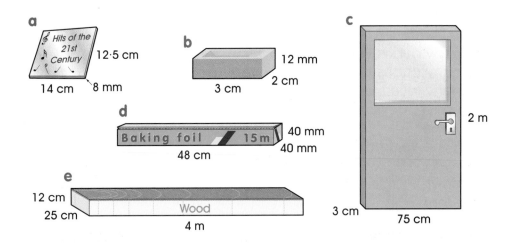

a Hits of the 21st Century
12·5 cm
14 cm   8 mm

b 12 mm
2 cm
3 cm

c 2 m
3 cm   75 cm

d Baking foil   15 m
40 mm
40 mm
48 cm

e 12 cm
25 cm
Wood
4 m

5. The two fishtanks have the same volume.

a Calculate the volume of the tanks.
b What is the length of the second tank?
c The water in tank A is 19 cm deep.
In tank B, the water is 20 cm deep.

Find the volume of water in each tank:
i in cm³   ii in litres.

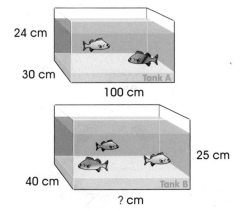

24 cm
30 cm
100 cm
Tank A

25 cm
40 cm
? cm
Tank B

6. The two packs of butter are the same price.
Which is the better bargain? Explain.

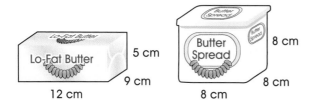

 B

1. Copy and complete the table. Where necessary, give answers rounded to
1 decimal place.

Cuboid	Length	Breadth	Height	Volume
A	8·5 cm	7 cm	2·5 cm	... cm³
B	64 cm	18 mm	5 mm	... cm³
C	3·5 cm	2·5 cm	2·5 cm	... cm³
D	18 m	12 cm	6·5 cm	... cm³
E	15 cm	... cm	6 cm	1260 cm³
F	24 m	16 m	... m	883·2 m³

2. A factory makes plastic dominoes.
Each domino is a solid cuboid with
dimensions as shown.

A block of plastic 50 cm by 30 cm by
25 cm is melted down and poured into
moulds. How many dominoes can be
made from the block?

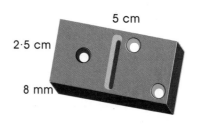

3. A square sheet of metal with side 3·5 metres is 12 millimetres thick.
Calculate its volume in cm³.

4. A children's paddling pool is in the shape of a cuboid.
It is 15 m long, 12 m broad and 25 cm deep.
Calculate its volume in:

a m³   **b** cm³   **c** litres.

5. Calculate the volume of the platform
by dividing it into two cuboids.

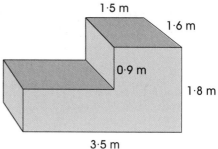

6. **a** Calculate the number of litres of water needed to fill this pool.
    b 1 litre of water weighs 1 kilogram. What is the weight of the water needed to fill the pool? Give your answer in tonnes.

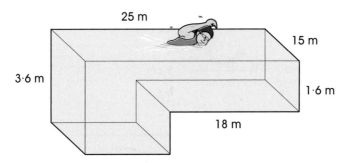

◆ Investigate

1. One litre of water (1000 cm³) fills a container
    10 cm by 10 cm by 10 cm.
    List the whole number dimensions of other cuboid containers
    that are filled by one litre of water.

2. You have a set of see-saw scales.

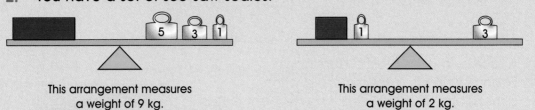

| This arrangement measures | This arrangement measures |
| a weight of 9 kg. | a weight of 2 kg. |

You need a set of weights that will weigh objects ranging from
1 kilogram to 39 kilograms, to the nearest kilogram.
What is the least number of weights you require and which ones are
they?

◆ Challenge

Speedie & Company have a van with a load-carrying space 4·3 m long,
1·5 m wide and 1·9 m high.

   a How many 2 m by 12 cm by 12 cm posts can be carried in it?
   b How many smaller posts, 1·8 m by 12 cm by 12 cm, can be put
         in the remaining space?

Two Dimensions

Within the structure of the Forth Bridge you can find examples of most of the quadrilaterals that you studied in Block 3.

This picture shows the bridge being built. Note how each section is being constructed symmetrically. this is not accidental.

1 Looking Back

1. Name the quadrilateral that:

   a has one axis of symmetry running along a diagonal
   b has four axes of symmetry
   c has a centre of symmetry but no axis of symmetry
   d has one pair of parallel sides
   e has two axes of symmetry cutting its sides
   f has four equal sides but no right angles.

2. What important angle property of the quadrilateral do we discover by examining a tiling made up of congruent quadrilaterals?

3. Calculate the size of the labelled angle in the quadrilateral ABCD:

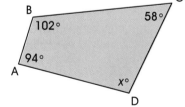

4. a Calculate the perimeter of the kite.
   b Calculate the angles of the rhombus.

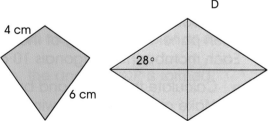

Challenge

James is doing a loft conversion.
A diagram of one wall is given.

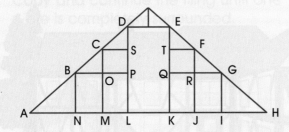

How many trapezia can
you name in the diagram?

B

1. Mary is making a model of the Forth Bridge using spaghetti.
    Here is one of the sections. It has two axes of symmetry.

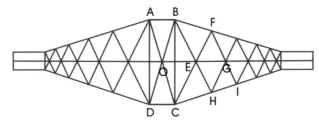

a   What kind of quadrilateral is: i ABCD   ii OBEC.
b   i   Given that lines which look parallel are parallel, EFGH is a
        parallelogram. Using this fact, what length is equal to EF?
    ii EG lies on the axis of symmetry, so EFGH is a kite.
        Using this fact, what length is equal to EF?
    iii What can you call a parallelogram that is also a kite?
c   i   What kind of shape is BFGH?
    ii Name a quadrilateral congruent to BFGH.

2. Thomas is also modelling a bridge.
    This is a diagram of one support.
    It has two axes of symmetry and
    lines that look parallel are parallel.

    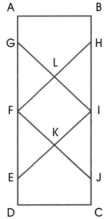

    a   ∠EKJ = 100°. Sketch the
        diagram and mark the size of
        as many angles as you can.
    b   What kind of quadrilateral is:
        i   ABCD   ii FLIK
        iii ABHF   iv FGIJ?
    c   Name a quadrilateral congruent to: i FGIJ   ii ABHF.

3. The cross-spar of the pylon is a trapezium.

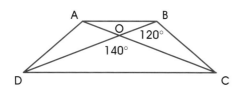

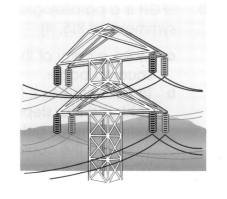

  a Name the parallel sides.
  b ∠DOC = 140°.
     Calculate the size of:
       i ∠AOD   ii ∠ODC   iii ∠OAB.
  c ∠OBC = 120°.
     Prove that AC cuts ∠DCB in half.

3 Point to Point

1. ABCD is a square.
   A, B and C have been plotted on the grid.

  a State the coordinates of A, B and C.
  b Calculate the coordinates of D.
  c Where do the diagonals of the square cross?
  d E is the point (5, 10). What kind of
     quadrilateral is ABCE?
  e What kind of quadrilateral is ABCF where F is
     the point:
       i   (5, 6)   ii   (5, 4)
       iii (6, 3)   iv   (3, 4)?

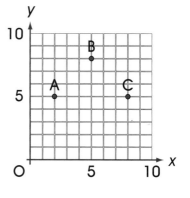

2. PQRS is a rhombus.
   The diagonal PR is double the length of the diagonal QS.
   Q is above S.

  a State the midpoint of PR.
  b Use this to help you figure out the
     coordinates of: i Q   and   ii S.

  c i   Find the coordinates of:
         A the midpoint of PQ,
         B the midpoint of QR,
         C the midpoint of RS
         D the midpoint of SP.
     ii What kind of quadrilateral is ABCD?

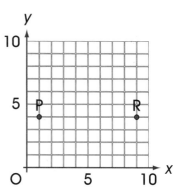

5. A doorway is a semicircle on top of a rectangle.

   a What is the diameter of the semicircle?
   b What is the circumference of the
      semicircle?
   c What is the perimeter of the door?

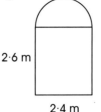

2·6 m

2·4 m

6. A bread bin has a side that is a quarter circle.
   It has a radius of 18 cm.

   a What is the diameter of the circle?
   b What is the circumference of the circle?
   c What is the length of the arc of the quarter circle?
   d What is the perimeter of the side of the bin?

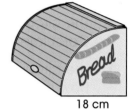

18 cm

Investigate

The formula **C = 3D** is only an approximation. It only gives rough answers.
It is true that the circumference is a multiple of the diameter, but this
multiple is a actually a decimal.

Can you find this multiple to two decimal places?

You could try to work it out by improved measuring,
or do some research on the Internet.

Unit 28 Three Dimensions

We live in a three-dimensional world full of three-dimensional shapes.

Architects everywhere use different 3-D shapes to design buildings.

Be aware of the different 3-D shapes in the buildings near you: cubes, cuboids, cylinders, spheres and many more.

1 Looking Back

1. Manufacturers use a variety of 3-D shapes (solids) to package their goods. Name the basic solid used in each of these:

2. Copy and complete this table :

	Solid	Faces	Vertices	Edges
a	Cuboid	6	8	12
b	Cube			
c	Square-based pyramid			
d	Triangular prism			
e	Cone			
f	Cylinder			
g	Sphere			

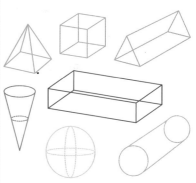

3. **a** Copy this representation of a cuboid on squared paper.
It represents the cuboid ABCDEFGH with
dimensions 4 units by 3 units by 2 units.

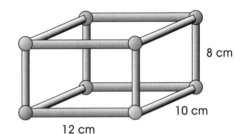

b In a similar way, draw a representation of a
cuboid with dimensions:

   i 2 by 5 by 2 units   ii 6 by 3 by 1 unit.

c In cuboid ABCDEFGH, name:

   i   the face congruent to ABCD
   ii the edges that are 2 cm in length
   iii three edges the same length as EF
   iv three edges that meet at vertex C
   v two faces that meet at the edge BC.

4. This is the skeleton model of a cuboid with
dimensions 8 cm × 10 cm × 12 cm.

   a How many straws are needed of length:

     i 8 cm   ii 10 cm   iii 12 cm?

   b How many red connectors are needed?

8 cm

10 cm

12 cm

5. A net is a pattern for making a solid.

   a Copy the net below onto squared paper and cut it out.

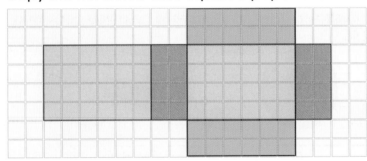

   b Fold it into a solid. What name is given to this solid?

6. **a** Here is the net of a cube.
Copy it onto squared paper
and construct the cube.
Each edge is 4 cm long.

   b The cube has eleven
different nets. Here
are two of them.
Check that they
indeed form
cubes.
Can you find the
eight other nets?

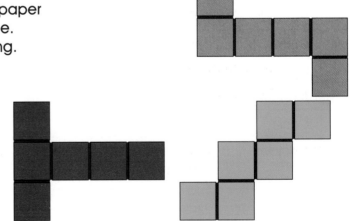

2 Prisms

If you were to slice through a solid you would get a cross-section.
A **prism** is a shape whose cross section remains the same along its length.

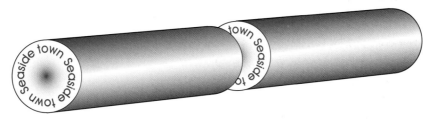

A stick of rock is a prism. Wherever you cut a stick of rock, you always see a circle with the name of the holiday resort written on it.

The prism takes its name from the name of the cross-section.

This house is a combination of a triangular prism and a rectangular prism (a cuboid).

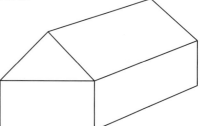

1. Some prisms are illustrated. Use the pictures to help you copy and complete the table.

	Name	Edges on end	Faces	Vertices	Edges
a	Triangular prism	3	5	6	9
b	Rectangular prism	4	6	8	12
c	Pentagonal prism				
d	Hexagonal prism				
e	Octagonal prism				
f	Circular prism				

From your completed table, you should see that if there are n edges on the end then there will be n + 2 faces.

$$F = n + 2$$

2. Find similar expressions in terms of *n* for:

   a V, the number of vertices
   b E, the number of edges.

3. A triangular prism has five faces, two are triangular and three rectangular.

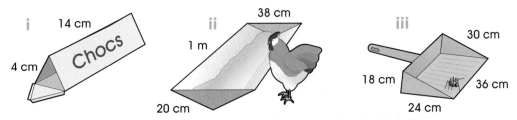

   a Prism i has an equiangular triangle (all the angles are equal) for a cross-section. Give the dimensions of the three rectangular faces.
   b The cross-section of the feeding trough ii is an isosceles triangle. What are the dimensions of the three rectangular faces (including the open face)?
   c In the case of the dust-pan, the cross-section is a right-angled triangle. What are the dimensions of the open face?

4. A tent is an isosceles triangular prism.

   a Plot the points A(2, 1), B(7, 2), C(11, 2), D(6, 1), E(4, 6) and F(9, 7).
   b Draw the quadrilateral ABCD. This represents the rectangular groundsheet.
   c Draw lines from:
      i A to E   ii D to E   iii B to F   iv C to F   v E to F.
      This represents the prism.
   d Name:
      i   a face congruent to DEFC
      ii   the two triangular faces
      iii the edges that meet at E
      iv   the faces that meet at the edge CD.

5. A prism has triangular faces that are equiangular.
   Each of the three rectangular faces is 3 cm by 5 cm.

   a Calculate the perimeter of the triangular faces.

      Hint There are two possible answers; one is illustrated.

   b With the aid of squared paper, make open-ended versions of both possible prisms.

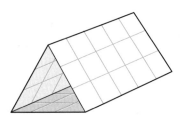

6. A table-top football game has goals as shown.

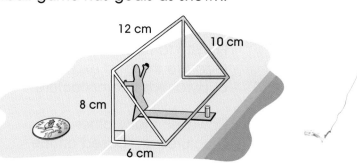

a Make the net of the goal.
There should be a rectangle for
the base and one for the back
but not one for the goal mouth.

b Make a model of the goal.

7. Here is the net of a triangular prism:

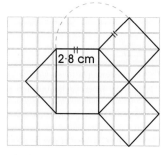

a Copy it onto squared paper.
b Make two copies of the model.
c Place the two copies together to make:
  i a right-triangular prism
  ii a cube.

◆ Investigate

The roof of a Swiss chalet is a triangular prism with an apex angle
less than 50°.
The roof of a house in the UK is likely to have an angle nearer 120°.
Think of the winter weather and suggest a practical reason for this
difference.

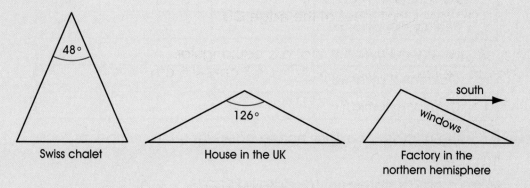

A factory in the northern hemisphere often has a roof that is a triangular
prism. The triangle has a longer side facing south, with windows on the
rectangular face. Why?

3 Pyramids

Egypt's famous pyramids at Giza are the best examples of pyramids in architecture.

However, many other structures are based on the pyramid. The Eiffel Tower is one. Can you find out about any others.

A pyramid has a base.
Edges rise from the vertices of the base to a single point called the **apex**.
The pyramid takes its name from the kind of base it has.

A

1. Name the following pyramids. The base has been highlighted.

a   b   c   d   e   f

2. **a** Copy and complete the table for the above shapes:

	Name	Edges on base	Faces	Vertices	Edges
a	Triangular pyramid	3	4	4	6
b	Rectangular pyramid	4	5	5	8
c	Pentagonal pyramid				
d	Hexagonal pyramid				
e	Octagonal pyramid				
f	Circular pyramid				

b If n is the number of edges on the base, then the number of faces is $F = n + 1$.

Make a similar statement to relate n to:
   i the number of vertices **V**
   ii the number of edges **E**.

c Use the formulae to work out the number of faces, vertices and edges to be counted in a pyramid with a base of 20 sides.

3. a Plot the points B(2, 2), C(5, 0) and D(9, 2). Join these to form a triangle.
   This will represent the base of a pyramid.
   b Plot the point A(5, 6) to represent the apex of the pyramid.
   Join A to each of the vertices of the base. Show the edges that are
   hidden by using dotted lines.

   **This is a 2-D picture of a triangular pyramid. It has four faces and
   is often called a tetrahedron from the Greek words tetra (four) and
   hedra (seat).**

4. a Plot the points E (1, 1), F (3, 2), G (7, 2), H (5, 1) and join them to
   represent a square base.
   b Plot apex I (4, 5). Join I to each vertex in the base.
   c Which edges meet at: i G   ii H?
   d Which faces meet at the edge EF?

5. a Plot the points J (3, 1), K (2, 3), L (5, 3), M (9, 3), N (8, 1).
   Join the points to make shape JKLMN.
   This is to represent the regular base of a pyramid.
   Name this 2-D shape.
   b Plot the apex P (5, 8) and join each vertex to it.
   Name the type of pyramid you have drawn.
   c Name the edges that intersect at M.
   d Name the faces that meet at the edge MP.

6. On his trip abroad, Mike had a meal on board
   the plane. His salt came in a small container
   whose net is shown.

   This net contains one square and four
   isosceles triangles.

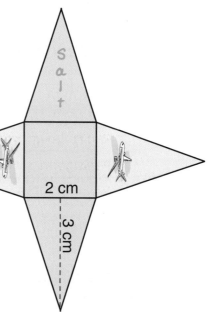

   a Make an accurate copy of the net.
   b Cut out and form the salt cellar.
   c Measure the length of the edges of the
     triangular faces to the nearest mm.

7. Helen's baby brother has a toy teepee which when built is a square-based pyramid. The base has a side of 1 m. 1·5 m rods rise up and are joined at the vertex. Sheeting is then put over the frame.

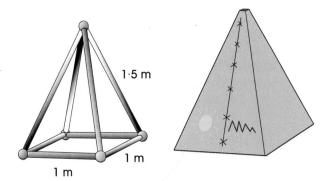

1·5 m

1 m

1 m

a   The maker lists all the contents on the box. Write out this list including:
   i   how many of each length of rod and how many connectors
   ii a description of the shapes making up the sheeting.

b   Sketch the net of the sheeting.

8. A regular tetrahedron is made from four equilateral triangles. The diagram shows how you can draw one with the aid of a set of compasses.

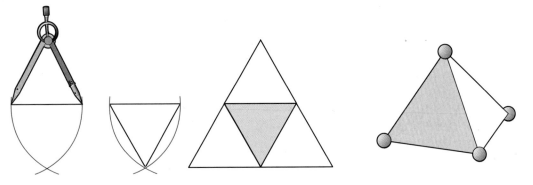

Make a regular tetrahedron of edge 10 cm.

Challenge

You have a 63 cm length of straw.

   a   What is the biggest regular tetrahedron you can construct?
   b   Draw the net of the tetrahedron.
   c   Make the tetrahedron and use this to design a Christmas decoration or a mobile.